ANNOUNCING THE F
NOW IN PREPARATION

MW00463754

The edition of *The Complete Works of Frances Ridley Havergal*

Volume I *Behold Your King:*
  The Complete Poetical Works of Frances Ridley Havergal

Volume II *Whose I Am and Whom I Serve:*
  Prose Works of Frances Ridley Havergal

Volume III *Loving Messages for the Little Ones:*
  Works for Children by Frances Ridley Havergal

Volume IV *Love for Love: Frances Ridley Havergal:*
  Memorials, Letters and Biographical Works

Volume V *Songs of Truth and Love:*
  Music by Frances Ridley Havergal and William Henry Havergal

David L. Chalkley, Editor   Dr. Glen T. Wegge, Music Editor

The Music of Frances Ridley Havergal by Glen T. Wegge, Ph.D.

This Companion Volume to the Havergal edition is a valuable presentation of F.R.H.'s extant scores. Except for a very few of her hymntunes published in hymnbooks, most or nearly all of F.R.H.'s scores have been very little—if any at all—seen, or even known of, for nearly a century. What a valuable body of music has been unknown for so long and is now made available to many. Dr. Wegge completed his Ph.D. in Music Theory at Indiana University at Bloomington, and his diligence and thoroughness in this volume are obvious. First an analysis of F.R.H.'s compositions is given, an essay that both addresses the most advanced musicians and also reaches those who are untrained in music; then all the extant scores that have been found are newly typeset, with complete texts for each score and extensive indices at the end of the book. This volume presents F.R.H.'s music in newly typeset scores diligently prepared by Dr. Wegge, and Volume V of the Havergal edition presents the scores in facsimile, the original 19th century scores. (The essay—a dissertation—analysing her scores is given the same both in this Companion Volume and in Volume V of the Havergal edition.)

  Dr. Wegge is also preparing all of these scores for publication in performance folio editions.

"Jesus Only."

Jesus Only! In the shadow
  Of the cloud so chill & dim,
We are clinging, loving, trusting,
  He with us & we with Him,
All unseen, though ever nigh,
Jesus Only - all our cry!

Jesus Only! In the glory,
  When the shadows all are flown,
Seeing Him in all His beauty,
  Satisfied with Him alone,
May we join His ransomed throng,
Jesus Only - all our song!

Frances Ridley Havergal
        July 4. 1876.

A poem by F.R.H., in her handwriting, a fair copy autograph. She wrote this on December 4, 1870, and apparently July 4, 1876 was the date when she wrote out this copy. Late in her life, the elderly Charles Henry Purday collaborated with her on a volume of music scores composed by him to poems by her, and his setting of "Jesus Only" was the first score in Songs of Peace and Joy. *See page iv.*

KEPT

FOR

THE MASTER'S USE.

AND

STARLIGHT THROUGH THE SHADOWS,

And Other Gleams from the King's Word.

BY

FRANCES RIDLEY HAVERGAL.

"Knowing her intense desire that Christ should be magnified, whether
by her life or in her death, may it be to His glory
that in these pages she, being dead,
'Yet speaketh ! ' "

Taken from the Edition of *The Complete Works of Frances Ridley Havergal.*

David L. Chalkley, Editor   Dr. Glen T. Wegge, Associate Editor

ISBN 978-1-937236-15-1   Library of Congress: 2011941555

Book cover by Sherry Goodwin and David Carter.

CONTENTS.

LIST OF ILLUSTRATIONS

This is the poem given in F.R.H.'s manuscript on page ii.

"Jesus Only."

Jesus Only! In the shadow
　　Of the cloud so chill and dim,
We are clinging, loving, trusting,
　　He with us and we with Him.
All unseen, though ever nigh,
Jesus Only – all our cry!

Jesus Only! In the glory
　　When the shadows all are flown,
Seeing Him in all His beauty,
　　Satisfied with Him alone,
May we join His ransomed throng,
Jesus Only – all our song!

KEPT

FOR

The Master's Use.

BY

FRANCES RIDLEY HAVERGAL.

"Thou shalt abide *for Me.*"—Hosea 3:3.

Hundred and Ninety-seventh Thousand.

London:
JAMES NISBET & CO. LIMITED
21 BERNERS STREET, W.

PREFATORY NOTE.

My beloved sister Frances finished revising the proofs of this book shortly before her death on Whit Tuesday, June 3, 1879, but its publication was to be deferred till the Autumn.

In appreciation of the deep and general sympathy flowing in to her relatives, they wish that its publication should not be withheld. Knowing her intense desire that Christ should be magnified, whether by her life or in her death, may it be to His glory that in these pages she, being dead,

"Yet speaketh!"

MARIA V. G. HAVERGAL.

OAKHAMPTON, WORCESTERSHIRE,
11*th June* 1879.

IT is the desire of nearest relatives to devote any profit arising from the sale of this book in erecting a MEMORIAL VESTRY AND SEATS FOR SIX-TY SUNDAY-SCHOOL CHILDREN at the Parish Church of which her only surviving brother is Incumbent. These improvements are not only desirable, but much needed. Such a building, with its attendant inscription, will be a lasting memorial to "*F. R. H.*"

Upton Bishop, near Ross
Herefordshire.

CONTENTS.

F.R.H.'s brother, Francis Tebbs Havergal (1829–1890), wrote this at the front of a copy of *Kept for the Master's Use:*

"Francis Tebbs Havergal Vicar of Upton Bishop 1879. August 1st."

"This copy was the only one ever seen by my dear sister Fanny. It was sent to her as a 'printer's proof' about the 24 of May 1879, just when her last illness commenced. She tied it up and left it on her desk. There I saw it and took possession of it by M.V.G.H.'s permission. I at once asked that profits might be devoted to Upton Church. A preface & note were written about June 12th and this book was published in July. It was my sister's intention to postpone its publication till the autumn, but the popular demand for it being so general no time was lost in putting it before the public."

TAKE my life, and let it be
Consecrated, Lord, to Thee.

Take my moments and my days;
Let them flow in ceaseless praise.

Take my hands, and let them move
At the impulse of Thy love.

Take my feet, and let them be
Swift and "beautiful" for Thee.

Take my voice, and let me sing
Always, only, for my King.

Take my lips, and let them be
Filled with messages from Thee.

Take my silver and my gold;
Not a mite would I withhold.

Take my intellect, and use
Every power as Thou shalt choose.

Take my will, and make it Thine;
It shall be no longer mine.

Take my heart, it *is* Thine own;
It shall be Thy royal throne.

Take my love; my Lord, I pour
At Thy feet its treasure-store.

Take myself, and I will be
Ever, *only*, ALL for Thee.

CHAPTER I.

Our Lives Kept for Jesus.

"*Keep my life, that it may be
Consecrated, Lord, to Thee.*"

M ANY a heart has echoed the little song:

"Take my life, and let it be
Consecrated, Lord, to Thee!"

And yet those echoes have not been, in every case and at all times, so clear, and full, and firm, so continuously glad as we would wish, and perhaps expected. Some of us have said:

"I launch me forth upon a sea
Of boundless love and tenderness";

and after a little we have found, or fancied, that there is a hidden leak in our barque, and though we are doubtless still afloat, yet we are not sailing with the same free, exultant confidence as at first. What is it that has dulled and weakened the echo of our consecration song? what is the little leak that hinders the swift and buoyant course of our consecrated life? Holy Father, let Thy loving Spirit guide the hand that writes, and strengthen the heart of every one who reads what shall be written, for Jesus' sake.

While many a sorrowfully-varied answer to these questions may, and probably will arise from touched and sensitive consciences, each being shown by God's faithful Spirit the special sin, the special yielding to temptation which has hindered and spoiled the blessed life which they sought to enter and enjoy, it seems to me that one or other of two things has lain at the outset of the failure and disappointment.

First, it may have arisen from want of the simplest belief in the simplest fact, as well as want of trust in one of the simplest and plainest words our gracious Master ever uttered! The unbelieved fact being simply that He hears us; the untrusted word being one of those plain, broad foundation-stones on which we rested our whole weight, it may be many years ago, and which we had no idea we ever doubted, or were in any danger of doubting now,—"Him that cometh to Me I will in no wise cast out."

"Take my life!" We have said it or sung it before the Lord, it may be many times; but if it were only once whispered in His ear with full purpose of heart, should we not believe that He heard it? And if we know that He heard it, should we not believe that He has answered it, and fulfilled this, our heart's desire? For with Him hearing means heeding. Then why should we doubt that He did verily take our lives when we offered them—our bodies when we presented them? Have we not been wronging His faithfulness all this time by practically, even if unconsciously, doubting whether the prayer ever really reached Him? And if so, is it any wonder that we have not realized all the power and joy of full consecration? By some means or other He has to teach us to trust implicitly at every step of the way. And so, if we did not really trust in this matter, He has had to let us find out our want of trust by withholding the sensible part of the blessing, and thus stirring us up to find out why it is withheld.

An offered gift must be either accepted or refused. Can He have refused it when He has said, "Him that cometh to Me I will in no wise cast out"? If not, then it must have been accepted. It is just the same process as when we came to Him first of all, with the intolerable burden of our sins. There was no help for it but to come with them to Him, and take His word for it that He would not and did not cast us out. And so coming, so believing, we found rest to our souls; we found that His word was true and that His taking away our sins was a reality.

Some give their lives to Him then and there, and go forth to live thenceforth not at all unto themselves, but unto Him who died for them. This is as it should be, for conversion and consecration ought to be simultaneous. But practically it is not very often so, except with those in whom the bringing out of darkness into marvellous light has been sudden and dazzling, and full of deepest contrasts. More frequently the work resembles the case of the Hebrew servant described in Exodus 21, who, after six years' experience of a good master's service, dedicates himself voluntarily, unreservedly, and irrevocably to it, saying, "I love my master; I will not go out free"; the master then accepting and sealing him to a life-long service, free in law, yet bound in love. This seems to be a figure of later consecration founded on experience and love.

And yet, as at our first coming, it is less than nothing, worse than nothing that we have to bring; for our lives, even our redeemed and pardoned lives, are not only weak and worthless, but defiled and sinful. But thanks be to God for the Altar that sanctifieth the gift, even our Lord Jesus Christ Himself! By Him we draw nigh unto God; to Him, as one with the Father, we offer our living sacrifice; in Him, as the Beloved of the Father, we know it is accepted. So, dear friends, when once He has wrought in us the desire to be altogether His own, and put into our hearts the prayer, "Take my life," let us go on our way rejoicing, believing that He *has* taken our lives, our hands, our feet, our voices, our intellects, our wills, our whole selves, to be ever, only, all for Him. Let us consider that a blessedly settled thing; not because of anything we have felt, or said, or done, but because we know that He heareth us, and because we know that He is true to His word.

But suppose our hearts do not condemn us in this matter, our disappointment may arise from another cause. It may be that we have not received, because we have not asked a fuller and further blessing. Suppose that we did believe, thankfully and surely, that the Lord heard our prayer, and that He did indeed answer and accept us, and set us apart for Himself; and yet we find that our consecration was not merely miserably incomplete, but that we have drifted back again almost to where we were before. Or suppose things are not quite so bad as that, still we have not quite all we expected; and even if we think we can truly say, "O God, my heart is fixed," we find that, to our daily sorrow, somehow or other the details of our conduct do not seem to be fixed, something or other is perpetually slipping through, till we get perplexed and distressed. Then we are tempted to wonder whether after all there was not some mistake about it, and the Lord did not really take us at our word, although we took Him at His word. And then the struggle with one doubt, and entanglement, and temptation only seems to land us in another. What is to be done then?

First, I think, very humbly and utterly honestly to search and try our ways before our God; or rather, as we shall soon realize our helplessness to make such a search, ask Him to do it for us, praying for His promised Spirit to show us unmistakeably if there is any secret thing with us that is hindering both the inflow and outflow of His grace to us and through us. Do not let us shrink from some unexpected flash into a dark corner; do not let us wince at the sudden touching of a hidden plague-spot. The Lord always does His own work thoroughly if we will only let Him do it; if we put our case into His hands, He will search and probe fully and firmly, though very tenderly. Very painfully, it may be, but only that He may do the very thing we want,—cleanse us and heal us thoroughly, so that we may set off to walk in real newness of life. But if we do not put it unreservedly into His hands, it will be no use thinking or talking about our lives being consecrated to Him. The heart that is not entrusted to Him for searching, will not be undertaken by Him for cleansing; the life that fears to come to the light lest any deed should be reproved, can never know the blessedness and the privileges of walking in the light.

But what then? When He has graciously again put a new song in our mouth, and we are singing,

> "Ransomed, healed, restored, forgiven,
> Who like me His praise should sing?"

and again with fresh earnestness we are saying,

> "Take my life, and let it be
> Consecrated, Lord, to Thee!"

are we only to look forward to the same disappointing experience over again? are we always to stand at the threshold? Consecration is not so much a step as a course; not so much an act, as a position to which a course of action inseparably belongs. In so far as it is a course and a position, there must naturally be a definite entrance upon it, and a time, it may be a moment, when that entrance is made. That is when we say, "Take"; but we do not want to go on taking a first step over and over again. What we want now is to be maintained in that position, and to fulfil that course. So let us go on to another prayer. Having already said, "Take my life, for I cannot give it to Thee," let us now say, with deepened conviction, that without Christ we really can do nothing,—"Keep my life, for I cannot keep it for Thee."

Let us ask this with the same simple trust to which, in so many other things, He has so liberally and graciously responded. For this is the confidence that we have in Him, that if we ask anything according to His will, He heareth us; and if we know that He hears us, whatsoever we ask, we know that we have the petitions that we desired of Him. There can be no doubt that this petition is according to His will, because it is based upon many a promise. May I give it you just as it floats through my own mind again and again, knowing whom I have believed, and being persuaded that He is *able to keep* that which I have committed unto Him?

> Keep my life, that it may be
> Consecrated, Lord, to Thee.

Keep my moments and my days;
Let them flow in ceaseless praise.

Keep my hands, that they may move
At the impulse of Thy love.

Keep my feet, that they may be
Swift and "beautiful" for Thee.

Keep my voice, that I may sing
Always, only, for my King.

Keep my lips, that they may be
Filled with messages from Thee.

Keep my silver and my gold;
Not a mite would I withhold.

Keep my intellect, and use
Every power as Thou shalt choose.

Keep my will, oh, keep it Thine!
For it is no longer mine.

Keep my heart; it is Thine own
It is now Thy royal throne.

Keep my love; my Lord, I pour
At Thy feet its treasure-store.

Keep myself that I may be
Ever, *only*, ALL for Thee.

Yes! He who is able and willing to take unto Himself, is no less able and willing to keep for Himself. Our willing offering has been made by His enabling grace, and this our King has "seen with joy." And now we pray "Keep this for ever in the imagination of the thoughts of the heart of Thy people" (1 Chronicles 29:17, 18).

This blessed "taking," once for all, which we may quietly believe as an accomplished fact, followed by the continual "keeping," for which He will be continually inquired of by us, seems analogous to the great washing by which we have part in Christ, and the repeated washing of the feet for which we need to be continually coming to Him. For with the deepest and sweetest consciousness that He has indeed taken our lives to be His very own, the need of His active and actual keeping of them in every detail and at every moment is most fully realized. But then we have the promise of our faithful God, "I the Lord *do* keep it, I will keep it night and day." The only question is, will we trust this promise, or will we not? If we do, we shall find it come true. If not, of course it will not be realized. For unclaimed promises are like uncashed cheques; they will keep us from bankruptcy, but not from want. But if not, *why* not? What right have we to pick out one of His faithful sayings, and say we don't expect Him to fulfil that? What defence can we bring, what excuse can we invent, for so doing?

If you appeal to experience against His faithfulness to His word, I will appeal to experience too, and ask you, did you ever *really trust* Jesus to fulfil any word of His to you, and find your trust deceived? As to the past experience of the details of your life not being kept for Jesus, look a little more closely at it, and you will find that though you may have asked, you did not trust. Whatever you did really trust Him to keep, He has kept, and the unkept things were never really entrusted. Scrutinize this past experience as you will, and it will only bear witness against your unfaithfulness, never against His absolute faithfulness.

Yet this witness must not be unheeded. We must not forget the things that are behind till they are confessed and forgiven. Let us now bring all this unsatisfactory past experience, and, most of all, the want of trust which has been the poison-spring of its course, to the precious blood of Christ, which cleanseth us, even us, from all sin, even this sin. Perhaps we never saw that we were not trusting Jesus as He deserves to be trusted; if so, let us wonderingly hate ourselves the more that we could be so trustless to such a Saviour, and so sinfully dark and stupid that we did not even see it. And oh, let us wonderingly love Him the more that He has been so patient and gentle with us, upbraiding not, though in our slow-hearted foolishness we have been grieving Him by this subtle unbelief; and then, by His grace, may we enter upon a new era of experience, our lives kept for Him more fully than ever before, because we trust Him more simply and unreservedly to keep them!

Here we must face a question, and perhaps a difficulty. Does it not almost seem as if we were at this point led to trusting to our trust, making everything hinge upon it, and thereby only removing a subtle dependence upon ourselves one step farther back, disguising instead of renouncing it? If Christ's keeping depends upon our trusting, and our continuing to trust depends upon ourselves, we are in no better or safer position than before, and shall only be landed in a fresh series of disappointments. The old story, something for the sinner to *do*, crops up again here, only with the ground shifted from "works" to trust. Said a friend to me, "I see now! I did trust Jesus to do everything else for me, but I thought that this trusting was something that *I* had got to do." And so, of course, what she "had got to do" had been a perpetual effort and frequent failure. We can no more trust and keep on trusting than we can do anything else of ourselves. Even in this it must be "Jesus only"; we are not to look to Him only to be the Author and Finisher of our faith, but we are to look to Him for all the intermediate fulfilment of the work of faith (2 Thessalonians 1:11); we must ask Him to go on fulfilling it in us, committing even this to His power.

> For we both may and must
> Commit our very faith to Him,
> Entrust to Him our trust.

What a long time it takes us to come down to the conviction, and still more to the realization of the fact that without Him we can do *nothing*, but that He must work *all* our works in us! This is the work of God, that ye believe in Him whom He has sent. And no less must it be the work of God that we go on believing, and that we go on trusting. Then, dear friends, who are longing to trust Him with unbroken and unwavering trust, cease the effort and drop the burdens and *now* entrust your trust to Him! He is just as well able to keep that as any other part of the complex lives which we want Him to take and keep for Himself. And oh, do not pass on content with the thought, "Yes, that is a good idea; perhaps I should find that a great help!" But, "Now, then, *do it*." It is no help to the sailor to see a flash of light across a dark sea, if he does not instantly steer accordingly.

Consecration is not a religiously selfish thing. If it sinks into that, it ceases to be consecration. We want our lives kept, not that we may feel happy, and be saved the distress consequent on wandering, and get the power with God and man, and all the other privileges linked with it. We shall have all this, because the lower is included in the higher; but our true aim, if the love of Christ constraineth us, will be far beyond this. Not for "me" at all, but "for Jesus"; not for my safety, but for His glory; not for my comfort, but for His joy; not that I may find rest, but that He may see the travail of His soul, and be satisfied! Yes, for *Him* I want to be kept. Kept for His sake; kept for His use; kept to be His witness; kept for His joy! Kept for Him, that in me He may show forth some tiny sparkle of His light and beauty; kept to do His will and His work in His own way; kept, it may be, to suffer for His sake; kept for Him, that He may do just what seemeth Him good with me; kept, so that no other lord shall have any more dominion over me, but that Jesus shall have all there is to have;—little enough, indeed, but not divided or diminished by any other claim. Is not this, O you who love the Lord—is not this worth living for, worth asking for, worth trusting for?

This is consecration, and I cannot tell you the blessedness of it. It is not the least use arguing with one who has had but a taste of its blessedness, and saying to him, "How can these things be?" It is not the least use starting all sorts of difficulties and theoretical suppositions about it with such a one, any more than it was when the Jews argued with the man who said, "One thing I know, that whereas I was blind, now I see." The Lord Jesus does take the life that is offered to Him, and He does keep the life for Himself that is entrusted to Him; but until the life is offered we cannot know the taking, and until the life is entrusted we cannot know or understand the keeping. All we can do is to say, "O taste and see!" and bear witness to the reality of Jesus Christ, and set to our seal that we have found Him true to His every word, and that we have proved Him able even to do exceeding abundantly above all we asked or thought. Why should we hesitate to bear this testimony? We have done nothing at all; we have, in all our efforts, only proved to ourselves, and perhaps to others, that we had no power either to give or keep our lives. Why should we not, then, glorify His grace by acknowledging that we have found Him so wonderfully and tenderly gracious and faithful in both taking and keeping as we never supposed or imagined? I shall never forget the smile and emphasis with which a poor working man bore this witness to his Lord. I said to him, "Well, H., we have a good Master, have we not?" "Ah," said he, "a deal better than ever *I* thought!" That summed up his experience, and so it will sum up the experience of every one who will but yield their lives wholly to the same good Master.

I cannot close this chapter without a word with those, especially my younger friends, who, although they have named the name of Christ, are saying, "Yes, this is all very well for some people, or for older people, but I am not ready for it; I can't say I see my way to this sort of thing." I am going to take the lowest ground for a minute, and appeal to *your* "past experience." Are you satisfied with your experience of the other "sort of thing"? Your pleasant pursuits, your harmless recreations, your nice occupations, even your improving ones, what fruit are you having from them? Your social intercourse, your daily talks and walks, your investments of all the time that remains to you over and above the absolute duties God may have given you, what fruit that shall remain have you from all this? Day after day passes on, and year after year, and what shall the harvest be? What is even the present return? Are you getting any real and lasting satisfaction out of it all? Are you not finding that things lose their flavour, and that you are spending your strength day after day for nought? that you are no more satisfied than you were a year ago—rather less so, if anything? Does not a sense of hollowness and weariness come over you as you go on in the same round, perpetually getting through things only to begin again? It cannot be otherwise. Over even the freshest and purest earthly fountains the Hand that never makes a mistake has written, "He that drinketh of this water shall thirst again." Look into your own heart and you will find a copy of that inscription already traced, "*Shall thirst again.*" And the characters are being deepened with every attempt to quench the inevitable thirst and weariness in life, which can only be satisfied and rested in full consecration to God. For "Thou hast made us *for Thyself,* and the heart never resteth till it findeth rest in Thee." To-day I tell you of a brighter and happier life, whose inscription is, "*Shall never thirst,*"—a life that is no dull round-and-round in a circle of unsatisfactorinesses, but a life that has found its true and entirely satisfactory centre, and set itself towards a shining and entirely satisfactory goal, whose brightness is cast over every step of the way. Will you not seek it?

Do not shrink, and suspect, and hang back from what it may involve, with selfish and unconfiding and ungenerous half-heartedness. Take the word of any who have willingly offered themselves unto the Lord, that the life of consecration is "a deal better than they thought!" Choose this day whom you will serve with real, thoroughgoing, whole-hearted service, and He will receive you; and you will find, as we have found, that He is such a good Master that you are satisfied with His goodness, and that you will never want to go out free. Nay, rather take His own word for it; see what He says: "If they obey and serve Him, they shall spend their days in prosperity, and their years in pleasures." You cannot possibly understand that till you are really *in* His service! For He does not give, nor even show, His wages before you enter it. And He says, "My servants shall sing for joy of heart." But you cannot try over that song to see what it is like, you cannot even read one bar of it, till your nominal or even promised service is exchanged for real and undivided consecration. But when He can call you "My servant," then you will find yourself singing for joy of heart, because He says you shall.

"And who, then, is willing to consecrate his service this day unto the Lord?"

"Do not startle at the term, or think, because you do not understand all it may include, you are therefore not qualified for it. I daresay it comprehends a great deal more than either you or I understand, but we can both enter into the spirit of it, and the detail will unfold itself as long as our probation shall last. Christ demands a hearty consecration in *will*, and He will teach us what that involves in *act*."

This explains the paradox that "full consecration" may be in one sense the act of a moment, and in another the work of a lifetime. It must be complete to be real, and yet if real, it is always incomplete; a point of rest, and yet a perpetual progression.

Suppose you make over a piece of ground to another person. You give it up, then and there, entirely to that other; it is no longer in your own possession; you no longer dig and sow, plant and reap, at your discretion or for your own profit. His occupation of it is total; no other has any right to an inch of it; it is his affair thenceforth what crops to arrange for and how to make the most of it. But his practical occupation of it may not appear all at once. There may be waste land which he will take into full cultivation only by degrees, space wasted for want of draining or by over fencing, and odd corners lost for want of enclosing; fields yielding smaller returns than they might because of hedgerows too wide and shady, and trees too many and spreading, and strips of good soil trampled into uselessness for want of defined pathways.

Just so is it with our lives. The transaction of, so to speak, making them over to God is definite and complete. But then begins the practical development of consecration. And here He leads on "softly, according as the children be able to endure." I do not suppose any one sees anything like all that it involves at the outset. We have not a notion what an amount of waste of power there has been in our lives; we never measured out the odd comers and the undrained bits, and it never occurred to us what good fruit might be grown in our straggling hedgerows, nor how the shade of our trees has been keeping the sun from the scanty crops. And so, season by season, we shall be sometimes not a little startled, yet always very glad, as we find that bit by bit the Master shows how much more may be made of our ground, how much more He is able to make of it than we did; and we shall be willing to work under Him and do exactly what He points out, even if it comes to cutting down a shady tree or clearing out a ditch full of pretty weeds and wild-flowers.

As the seasons pass on, it will seem as if there was always more and more to be done; the very fact that He is constantly showing us something more to be done in it, proving it is really His ground. Only let Him *have* the ground, no matter how poor or overgrown the soil may be, and then "He will make her wilderness like Eden, and her desert like the garden of the Lord." Yes, even *our* "desert!" And then we shall sing, "My beloved is gone down into *His* garden, to the beds of spices, to feed in the gardens and to gather lilies."

Made for Thyself, O God!
Made for Thy love, Thy service, Thy delight;
Made to show forth Thy wisdom, grace, and might;
Made for Thy praise, whom veiled archangels laud:
Oh, strange and glorious thought, that we may be
A joy to Thee!

Yet the heart turns away
From this grand destiny of bliss, and deems
'Twas made for its poor self, for passing dreams,
Chasing illusions melting day by day,
Till for ourselves we read on this world's best,
"This is not rest!"

CHAPTER II.

Our Moments Kept for Jesus.

"Keep my moments and my days;
Let them flow in ceaseless praise."

IT may be a little help to writer and reader if we consider some of the practical details of the life which we desire to have "kept for Jesus" in the order of the little hymn at the beginning of this book, with the one word "take" changed to "keep." So we will take a couplet for each chapter.

The first point that naturally comes up is that which is almost synonymous with life—our time. And this brings us at once face to face with one of our past difficulties, and its probable cause.

When we take a wide sweep, we are so apt to be vague. When we are aiming at generalities we do not hit the practicalities. We forget that faithfulness to principle is only proved by faithfulness in detail. Has not this vagueness had something to do with the constant ineffectiveness of our feeble desire that our time should be devoted to God?

In things spiritual, the greater does not always include the less, but, paradoxically, the less more often includes the greater. So in this case, time is entrusted to us to be traded with for our Lord. But we cannot grasp it as a whole. We instinctively break it up ere we can deal with it for any purpose. So when a New Year comes round, we commit it with special earnestness to the Lord. But as we do so, are we not conscious of a feeling that even a year is too much for us to deal with? And does not this feeling, that we are dealing with a larger thing than we can grasp, take away from the sense of reality? Thus we are brought to a more manageable measure; and as the Sunday mornings or the Monday mornings come round, we thankfully commit the opening week to Him, and the sense of help and rest is renewed and strengthened. But not even the six or seven days are close enough to our hand; even to-morrow exceeds our tiny grasp, and even to-morrow's grace is therefore not given to us. So we find the need of considering our lives as a matter of day by day, and that any more general committal and consecration of our time does not meet the case so truly. Here we have found much comfort and help, and if results have not been entirely satisfactory, they have, at least, been more so than before we reached this point of subdivision.

But if we have found help and blessing by going a certain distance in one direction, is it not probable we shall find more if we go farther in the same? And so, if we may commit the days to our Lord, why not the hours, and why not the moments? And may we not expect a fresh and special blessing in so doing?

We do not realize the importance of moments. Only let us consider those two sayings of God about them, "In a moment shall they die," and, "We shall all be changed in a moment," and we shall think less lightly of them. Eternal issues may hang upon any one of them, but it has come and gone before we can even think about it. Nothing seems less within the possibility of our own keeping, yet nothing is more inclusive of all other keeping. Therefore let us ask Him to keep them for us.

Are they not the tiny joints in the harness through which the darts of temptation pierce us? Only give us time, we think, and we should not be overcome. Only give us time, and we could pray and resist, and the devil would flee from us! But he comes all in a moment; and in a moment—an unguarded, unkept one—we utter the hasty or exaggerated word, or think the un-Christ-like thought, or feel the un-Christ-like impatience or resentment.

But even if we have gone so far as to say, "Take my moments," have we gone the step farther, and really *let* Him take them—really entrusted them to Him? It is no good saying "take," when we do not let go. How can another keep that which we are keeping hold of? So let us, with full trust in His power, first commit these slippery moments to Him,—put them right into His hand,—and then we may trustfully and happily say, "Lord, keep them for me! Keep every one of the quick series as it arises. I cannot keep them for Thee; do Thou keep them for Thyself!"

But the sanctified and Christ-loving heart cannot be satisfied with only negative keeping. We do not want only to be kept from displeasing Him, but to be kept always pleasing Him. Every "kept *from*" should have its corresponding and still more blessed "kept *for*." We do not want our moments to be simply kept from Satan's use, but kept for His use; we want them to be not only kept from sin, but kept for His praise.

Do you ask, "But what use can He make of mere moments?" I will not stay to prove or illustrate the obvious truth that, as are the moments so will be the hours and the days which they build. You understand that well enough. I will answer your question as it stands.

Look back through the history of the Church in all ages, and mark how often a great work and mighty influence grew out of a mere moment in the life of one of God's servants; a mere moment, but overshadowed and filled with the fruitful power of the Spirit of God. The moment may have been spent in uttering five words, but they have fed five thousand, or even five hundred thousand. Or it may have been lit by the flash of a thought that has shone into hearts and homes throughout the land, and kindled torches that have been borne into earth's darkest corners. The rapid speaker or the lonely thinker little guessed what use his Lord was making of that single moment. There was no room in it for even a thought of that. If that moment had not been, though perhaps unconsciously, "kept for Jesus," but had been otherwise occupied, what a harvest to His praise would have been missed!

The same thing is going on every day. It is generally a moment—either an opening or a culminating one—that really does the work. It is not so often a whole sermon as a single short sentence in it that wings God's arrow to a heart. It is seldom a whole conversation that is the means of bringing about the desired result, but some sudden turn of thought or word, which comes with the electric touch of God's power. Sometimes it is less than that; only a look (and what is more momentary?) has been used by Him for the pulling down of strongholds. Again, in our own quiet waiting upon God, as moment after moment glides past in the silence at His feet, the eye resting upon a page of His Word, or only looking up to Him through the darkness, have we not found that He can so irradiate one passing moment with His light that its rays never die away, but shine on and on through days and years? Are not such moments proved to have been kept for Him? And if some, why not all?

This view of moments seems to make it clearer that it is impossible to serve two masters, for it is evident that the service of a moment cannot be divided. If it is occupied in the service of self, or any other master, it is not at the Lord's disposal; He cannot make use of what is already occupied.

Oh, how much we have missed by not placing them at His disposal! What might He not have done with the moments freighted with self or loaded with emptiness, which we have carelessly let drift by! Oh, what might have been if they had all been kept for Jesus! How He might have filled them with His light and life, enriching our own lives that have been impoverished by the waste, and using them in far-spreading blessing and power!

While we have been undervaluing these fractions of eternity, what has our gracious God been doing in them? How strangely touching are the words, "What is man, that Thou shouldest set Thine heart upon him, and that Thou shouldest visit him every morning, *and try him every moment?*" Terribly solemn and awful would be the thought that He has been trying us every moment, were it not for the yearning gentleness and love of the Father revealed in that wonderful expression of wonder, "What is man, that Thou shouldest set Thine heart upon him?" Think of that ceaseless setting of His heart upon us, careless and forgetful children as we have been! And then think of those other words, none the less literally true because given under a figure: "I, the Lord, do keep it; *I will water it every moment.*"

We see something of God's infinite greatness and wisdom when we try to fix our dazzled gaze on infinite space. But when we turn to the marvels of the microscope, we gain a clearer view and more definite grasp of these attributes by gazing on the perfection of His infinitesimal handiworks. Just so, while we cannot realize the infinite love which fills eternity, and the infinite vistas of the great future are "dark with excess of light" even to the strongest telescopes of faith, we see that love magnified in the microscope of the moments, brought very close to us, and revealing its unspeakable perfection of detail to our wondering sight.

But we do not see this as long as the moments are kept in our own hands. We are like little children closing our fingers over diamonds. How can they receive and reflect the rays of light, analyzing them into all the splendour of their prismatic beauty, while they are kept shut up tight in the dirty little hands? Give them up; let our Father hold them for us, and throw His own great light upon them, and then we shall see them full of fair colours of His manifold loving-kindnesses; and let Him always keep them for us, and then we shall always see His light and His love reflected in them.

And then, surely, they shall be filled with praise. Not that we are to be always singing hymns, and using the expressions of other people's praise, any more than the saints in glory are always literally singing a new song. But praise will be the tone, the colour, the atmosphere in which they flow; none of them away from it or out of it.

Is it a little too much for them all to "flow in ceaseless praise"? Well, where will you stop? What proportion of your moments do you think enough for Jesus? How many for the spirit of praise, and how many for the spirit of heaviness? Be explicit about it, and come to an understanding. If He is not to have all, then *how much?* Calculate, balance, and apportion. You will not be able to do this in heaven—you know it will be all praise there; but you are free to halve your service of praise here, or to make the proportion what you will.

Yet,—He made you for His glory.

Yet,—He chose you that you should be to the praise of His glory.

Yet,—He loves you every moment, waters you every moment, watches you unslumberingly, cares for you unceasingly.

Yet,—He died for you!

Dear friends, one can hardly write it without tears. Shall you or I remember all this love, and hesitate to give all our moments up to Him? Let us entrust Him with them, and ask Him to keep them all, every single one, for His own beloved self, and fill them *all* with His praise, and let them *all* be to His praise!

CHAPTER III.

Our Hands Kept for Jesus.

*"Keep my hands, that they may move
At the impulse of Thy love."*

WHEN the Lord has said to us, "Is thine heart right, as My heart is with thy heart?" the next word seems to be, "If it be, give Me thine hand."

What a call to confidence, and love, and free, loyal, happy service is this! and how different will the result of its acceptance be from the old lamentation: "We labour and have no rest; we have given the hand to the Egyptians and to the Assyrians." In the service of these "other lords," under whatever shape they have presented themselves, we shall have known something of the meaning of having "both the hands full with travail and vexation of spirit." How many a thing have we "taken in hand," as we say, which we expected to find an agreeable task, an interest in life, a something towards filling up that unconfessed "aching void" which is often most real when least acknowledged; and after a while we have found it change under our hands into irksome travail, involving perpetual vexation of spirit! The thing may have been of the earth and for the world, and then no wonder it failed to satisfy even the instinct of work, which comes natural to many of us. Or it may have been right enough in itself, something for the good of others so far as we understood their good, and unselfish in all but unravelled motive, and yet we found it full of tangled vexations, because the hands that held it were not simply consecrated to God. Well, if so, let us bring these soiled and tangle-making hands to the Lord, "Let us lift up our heart with our hands" to Him, asking Him to clear and cleanse them.

If He says, "What is that in thine hand?" let us examine honestly whether it is something which He can use for His glory or not. If not, do not let us hesitate an instant about dropping it. It may be something we do not like to part with; but the Lord is able to give thee much more than this, and the first glimpse of the excellency of the knowledge of Christ Jesus your Lord will enable us to count those things loss which were gain to us.

But if it is something which He can use, He will make us do ever so much more with it than before. Moses little thought what the Lord was going to make him do with that "rod in his hand"! The first thing he had to do with it was to "cast it on the ground," and see it pass through a startling change. After this he was commanded to take it up again, hard and terrifying as it was to do so. But when it became again a rod in his hand, it was no longer what it was before, the simple rod of a wandering desert shepherd. Henceforth it was "the rod of God in his hand" (Exodus 4:20), wherewith he should do signs, and by which God Himself would do "marvellous things" (Psalm 78:12).

If we look at any Old Testament text about consecration, we shall see that the marginal reading of the word is, "fill the hand" (*e.g.* Exodus 28:41; 1 Chronicles 29:5). Now, if our hands are full of "other things," they cannot be filled with "the things that are Jesus Christ's"; there must be emptying before there can be any true filling. So if we are sorrowfully seeing that our hands have not been kept for Jesus, let us humbly begin at the beginning, and ask Him to empty them thoroughly, that He may fill them completely.

For they *must* be emptied. Either we come to our Lord willingly about it, letting Him unclasp their hold, and gladly dropping the glittering weights they have been carrying, or, in very love, He will have to force them open, and wrench from the reluctant grasp the "earthly things" which are so occupying them that He cannot have His rightful use of them. There is only one other alternative, a terrible one,—to be let alone till the day comes when not a gentle Master, but the relentless king of terrors shall empty the trembling hands as our feet follow him out of the busy world into the dark valley, for "it is certain we can carry nothing out."

Yet the emptying and the filling are not all that has to be considered. Before the hands of the priests could be filled with the emblems of consecration, they had to be laid upon the emblem of atonement (Leviticus 8:14, *etc.*). That came first. "Aaron and his sons laid their hands upon the head of the bullock for the sin offering." So the transference of guilt to our Substitute, typified by that act, must precede the dedication of ourselves to God.

> "My faith would lay her hand
>   On that dear head of Thine,
> While like a penitent I stand,
>   And there confess my sin."

The blood of that Holy Substitute was shed "to make reconciliation upon the altar." Without that reconciliation we cannot offer and present ourselves to God; but this being made, Christ Himself presents us. And you, that were sometime alienated, and enemies in your mind by wicked works, yet now hath He reconciled in the body of His flesh through death, to present you holy and unblameable and unreprovable in His sight.

Then Moses "brought the ram for the burnt-offering; and Aaron and his sons laid their hands upon the head of the ram, and Moses burnt the whole ram upon the altar; it was a burnt-offering for a sweet savour, and an offering made by fire unto the Lord." Thus Christ's offering was indeed a whole one, body, soul, and spirit, each and all suffering even unto death, These atoning sufferings, accepted by God for us, are, by our own free act, accepted by us as the ground of our acceptance.

Then, reconciled and accepted, we are ready for consecration; for then "he brought the other ram, the ram of consecration; and Aaron and his sons laid their hands upon the head of the ram." Here we see Christ, "who is consecrated for evermore." We enter by faith into union with Him who said, "For their sakes I sanctify Myself, that they also might be sanctified through the truth."

After all this, their hands were filled with "consecrations for a sweet savour," so, after laying the hand of our faith upon Christ, suffering and dying for us, we are to lay that very same hand of faith, and in the very same way, upon Him as consecrated for us, to be the source and life and power of our consecration. And then our hands shall be filled with "consecrations," filled with Christ, and filled with all that is a sweet savour to God in Him.

"And who then is willing to fill his hand this day unto the Lord?" Do you want an added motive? Listen again: "Fill your hands to-day to the Lord, that He may bestow upon you a blessing this day." Not a long time hence, not even to-morrow, but "this day." Do you not want a blessing? Is not your answer to your Father's "What wilt thou?" the same as Achsah's, "Give me a blessing!" Here is His promise of just what you so want; will you not gladly fulfil His condition? A blessing shall immediately follow. He does not specify what it shall be; He waits to reveal it. You will find it such a blessing as you had not supposed could be for you—a blessing that shall verily make you rich, with no sorrow added—a blessing *this day*.

All that has been said about consecration applies to our literal members. Stay a minute, and look at your hand, the hand that holds this little book as you read it. See how wonderfully it is made; how perfectly fitted for what it has to do; how ingeniously connected with the brain, so as to yield that instantaneous and instinctive obedience without which its beautiful mechanism would be very little good to us! *Your* hand, do you say? Whether it is soft and fair with an easy life, or rough and strong with a working one, or white and weak with illness, it is the Lord Jesus Christ's. It is not your own at all; it belongs to Him. He made it, for without Him was not anything made that was made, not even your hand. And He has the added right of purchase—He has bought it that it might be one of His own instruments. We know this very well, but have we realized it? Have we really let Him have the use of these hands of ours? and have we ever simply and sincerely asked Him to keep them for His own use?

Does this mean that we are always to be doing some definitely "religious" work, as it is called? No, but that *all that we do* is to be always definitely done *for Him*. There is a great difference. If the hands are indeed moving "at the impulse of His love," the simplest little duties and acts are transfigured into holy service to the Lord.

> "A servant with this clause
>   Makes drudgery divine;
> Who sweeps a room as for Thy laws,
>   Makes that and the action fine."

George Herbert.

A Christian school-girl loves Jesus; she wants to please Him all day long, and so she practises her scales carefully and conscientiously. It is at the impulse of His love that her fingers move so steadily through the otherwise tiresome exercises. Some day her Master will find a use for her music; but meanwhile it may be just as really done unto Him as if it were Mr. Sankey at his organ, swaying the hearts of thousands. The hand of a Christian lad traces his Latin verses, or his figures, or his copying. He is doing his best, because a banner has been given him that it may be displayed, not so much by talk as by continuance in well-doing. And so, for Jesus' sake, his hand moves accurately and perseveringly.

A busy wife, or daughter, or servant has a number of little manual duties to perform. If these are done slowly and leisurely, they may be got through, but there will not be time left for some little service to the poor, or some little kindness to a suffering or troubled neighbour, or for a little quiet time alone with God and His word. And so the hands move quickly, impelled by the loving desire for service or communion, kept in busy motion for Jesus' sake. Or it may be that the special aim is to give no occasion of reproach to some who are watching, but so to adorn the doctrine that those may be won by the life who will not be won by the word. Then the hands will have their share to do; they will move carefully, neatly, perhaps even elegantly, making everything around as nice as possible, letting their intelligent touch be seen in the details of the home, and even of the dress, doing or arranging all the little things decently and in order for Jesus' sake. And so on with every duty in every position.

It may seem an odd idea, but a simple glance at one's hand, with the recollection, "This hand is not mine; it has been given to Jesus, and it must be kept for Jesus," may sometimes turn the scale in a doubtful matter, and be a safeguard from certain temptations. With that thought fresh in your mind as you look at your hand, can you let it take up things which, to say the very least, are not "for Jesus"? things which evidently cannot be used, as they most certainly are not used, either for Him or by Him? Cards, for instance! Can you deliberately hold in it books of a kind which you know perfectly well, by sadly repeated experience, lead you farther from instead of nearer to Him? books which must and do fill your mind with those "other things" which, entering in, choke the word? books which you would not care to read at all, if your heart were burning within you at the coming of His feet to bless you? Next time any temptation of this sort approaches, just *look at your hand!*

It was of a literal hand that our Lord Jesus spoke when He said, "Behold, the hand of him that betrayeth Me is with Me on the table"; and, "He that dippeth his hand with Me in the dish, the same shall betray Me." A hand so near to Jesus, with Him on the table, touching His own hand in the dish at that hour of sweetest, and closest, and most solemn intercourse, and yet betraying Him! That same hand taking the thirty pieces of silver! What a tremendous lesson of the need of keeping for our hands! Oh that every hand that is with Him at His sacramental table, and that takes the memorial bread, may be kept from any faithless and loveless motion! And again, it was by literal "wicked hands" that our Lord Jesus was crucified and slain. Does not the thought that human hands have been so treacherous and cruel to our beloved Lord, make us wish the more fervently that our hands may be totally faithful and devoted to Him?

Danger and temptation to let the hands move at other impulses is every bit as great to those who have nothing else to do but to render direct service, and who think they are doing nothing else. Take one practical instance—our letter-writing. Have we not been tempted (and fallen before the temptation), according to our various dispositions, to let the hand that holds the pen move at the impulse to write an unkind thought of another; or to say a clever and sarcastic thing, or a slightly coloured and exaggerated thing, which will make our point more telling; or to let out a grumble or a suspicion; or to let the pen run away with us into flippant and trifling words, unworthy of our high and holy calling?

Have we not drifted away from the golden reminder, "Should he reason with unprofitable talk, and with speeches wherewith he can do no good?" Why has this been, perhaps again and again? Is it not for want of putting our hands into our dear Master's hand, and asking and trusting Him to keep them? He *could* have kept; He *would* have kept!

Whatever our work or our special temptations may be, the principle remains the same, only let us apply it for ourselves.

Perhaps one hardly needs to say that the kept hands will be very gentle hands. Quick, angry motions of the heart will sometimes force themselves into expression by the hand, though the tongue may be restrained. The very way in which we close a door or lay down a book may be a victory or a defeat, a witness to Christ's keeping or a witness that we are not truly being kept. How can we expect that God will use this member as an instrument of righteousness unto Him, if we yield it thus as an instrument of unrighteousness unto sin? Therefore let us see to it, that it is at once yielded to Him whose right it is; and let our sorrow that it should have been even for an instant desecrated to Satan's use, lead us to entrust it henceforth to our Lord, to be kept by the power of God through faith "for the Master's use."

For when the gentleness of Christ dwells in us, He can use the merest touch of a finger. Have we not heard of one gentle touch on a wayward shoulder being the turning-point of a life? I have known a case in which the Master made use of less than that—only the quiver of a little finger being made the means of touching a wayward heart.

What must the touch of the Master's own hand have been! One imagines it very gentle though so full of power. Can He not communicate both the power and the gentleness? When He touched the hand of Peter's wife's mother, she arose and ministered unto them. Do you not think the hand which Jesus had just touched must have ministered very excellently? As we ask Him to "touch our lips with living fire," so that they may speak effectively for Him, may we not ask Him to touch our hands, that they may minister effectively, and excel in all that they find to do for Him? Then our hands shall be made strong by the hands of the Mighty God of Jacob.

It is very pleasant to feel that if our hands are indeed our Lord's, we may ask Him to guide them, and strengthen them, and teach them. I do not mean figuratively, but quite literally. In everything they do for Him (and that should be *everything we ever undertake*) we want to do it well—better and better. "Seek that ye may excel." We are too apt to think that He has given us certain natural gifts, but has nothing practically to do with the improvement of them, and leaves us to ourselves for that. Why not ask Him to make these hands of ours more handy for His service, more skilful in what is indicated as the "next thynge" they are to do? The "kept" hands need not be clumsy hands. If the Lord taught David's hands to war and his fingers to fight, will He not teach our hands, and fingers too, to do what He would have them do?

The Spirit of God must have taught Bezaleel's hands as well as his head, for he was filled with it not only that he might devise cunning works, but also in cutting of stones and carving of timber. And when all the women that were wise-hearted did spin with their hands, the hands must have been made skilful as well as the hearts made wise to prepare the beautiful garments and curtains.

There is a very remarkable instance of the hand of the Lord, which I suppose signifies in that case the power of His Spirit, being upon the hand of a man. In 1 Chronicles 28:19, we read: "All this, said David, the Lord made me understand in writing by His hand upon me, even all the works of this pattern." This cannot well mean that the Lord gave David a miraculously written scroll, because, a few verses before, it says that he had it all by the Spirit. So what else can it mean but that as David wrote, the hand of the Lord was upon his hand, impelling him to trace, letter by letter, the right words of description for all the details of the temple that Solomon should build, with its courts and chambers, its treasuries and vessels? Have we not sometimes sat down to write, feeling perplexed and ignorant, and wishing some one were there to tell us what to say? At such a moment, whether it were a mere note for post, or a sheet for press, it is a great comfort to recollect this mighty laying of a Divine hand upon a human one, and ask for the same help from the same Lord. It is sure to be given!

And now, dear friend, what about your own hands? Are they consecrated to the Lord who loves you? And if they are, are you trusting Him to keep them, and enjoying all that is involved in that keeping? Do let this be settled with your Master before you go on to the next chapter.

After all, this question will hinge on another, Do you love Him? If you really do, there can surely be neither hesitation about yielding them to Him, nor about entrusting them to Him to be kept. *Does He love you?* That is the truer way of putting it; for it is not our love to Christ, but the love of Christ to us which constraineth us. And this is the impulse of the motion and the mode of the keeping. The steam-engine does not move when the fire is not kindled, nor when it is gone out; no matter how complete the machinery and abundant the fuel, cold coals will neither set it going nor keep it working. Let us ask Him so to shed abroad His love in our hearts by the Holy Ghost which is given unto us, that it may be the perpetual and only impulse of every action of our daily life.

CHAPTER IV.

Our Feet Kept for Jesus.

"Keep my feet, that they may be
Swift and beautiful for Thee."

THE figurative keeping of the feet of His saints, with the promise that when they run they shall not stumble, is a most beautiful and helpful subject. But it is quite distinct from the literal keeping for Jesus of our literal feet.

There is a certain homeliness about the idea which helps to make it very real. These very feet of ours are purchased for Christ's service by the precious drops which fell from His own torn and pierced feet upon the cross. They are to be His errand-runners. How can we let the world, the flesh, and the devil have the use of what has been purchased with such payment?

Shall "the world" have the use of them? Shall they carry us where the world is paramount, and the Master cannot be even named, because the mention of His Name would be so obviously out of place? I know the apparent difficulties of a subject which will at once occur in connection with this, but they all vanish when our bright banner is loyally unfurled, with its motto, *"All* for Jesus!" Do you honestly want your very feet to be "kept for Jesus"? Let these simple words, *"Kept for Jesus,"* ring out next time the dancing difficulty or any other difficulty of the same kind comes up, and I know what the result will be!

Shall "the flesh" have the use of them? Shall they carry us hither and thither merely because we like to go, merely because it pleases ourselves to take this walk or pay this visit? And after all, what a failure it is! If people only *would* believe it, self-pleasing is always a failure in the end. Our good Master gives us a reality and fulness of *pleasure* in pleasing Him which we never get out of pleasing ourselves.

Shall "the devil" have the use of them? Oh no, of course not! We start back at this, as a highly unnecessary question. Yet if Jesus has not, Satan has.

For as all are serving either the Prince of Life or the prince of this world, and as no man can serve two masters, it follows that if we are not serving the one, we are serving the other. And Satan is only too glad to disguise this service under the less startling form of the world, or the still less startling one of self. All that is not "kept for Jesus," is left for self or the world, and therefore for Satan.

There is no fear but that our Lord will have many uses for what is kept by Him for Himself. "How beautiful are the feet of them that bring glad tidings of good things!" That is the best use of all; and I expect the angels think those feet beautiful, even if they are cased in muddy boots or goloshes.

Once the question was asked, "Wherefore wilt thou run, my son, seeing that thou hast no tidings ready?" So if we want to have these beautiful feet, we must have the tidings ready which they are to bear. Let us ask Him to keep our hearts so freshly full of His good news of salvation, that our mouths may speak out of their abundance. "If the clouds be full of rain, they empty themselves upon the earth." The "two olive branches empty the golden oil out of themselves." May we be so filled with the Spirit that we may thus have much to pour out for others!

Besides the great privilege of carrying water from the wells of salvation, there are plenty of cups of cold water to be carried in all directions; not to the poor only,—ministries of love are often as much needed by a rich friend. But the feet must be kept for these; they will be too tired for them if they are tired out for self-pleasing. In such services we are treading in the blessed steps of His most holy life, who "went about doing good."

Then there is literal errand-going,—just to fetch something that is needed for the household, or something that a tired relative wants, whether asked or unasked. Such things should come first instead of last, because these are clearly indicated as our Lord's will for us to do, by the position in which He has placed us; while what *seems* more direct service, may be after all not so directly apportioned by Him. "I have to go and buy some soap," said one with a little sigh. The sigh was waste of breath, for her feet were going to do her Lord's will for that next half-hour much more truly than if they had carried her to her well-worked district, and left the soap to take its chance.

A member of the Young Women's Christian Association wrote a few words on this subject, which, I think, will be welcome to many more than she expected them to reach:—

"May it not be a comfort to those of us who feel we have not the mental or spiritual power that others have, to notice that the living sacrifice mentioned in Romans 12:1 is our 'bodies'? Of course, that includes the mental power, but does it not also include the loving, sympathizing glance, the kind, encouraging word, *the ready errand for another*, the work of our hands, opportunities for all of which come oftener in the day than for the mental power we are often tempted to envy? May we be enabled to offer willingly that which we have." For if there be first a willing mind, it is accepted according to that a man hath, and not according to that he hath not.

If our feet are to be kept at His disposal, our eyes must be ever toward the Lord for guidance. We must look to Him for our orders where to go. Then He will be sure to give them. "The steps of a good man are ordered by the Lord." Very often we find that they have been so very literally ordered for us that we are quite astonished,—just as if He had not promised!

Do not smile at a *very* homely thought! If our feet are not our own, ought we not to take care of them for Him whose they are? Is it quite right to be reckless about "getting wet feet," which might be guarded against either by fore-thought or afterthought, when there is, at least, a risk of hindering our service thereby? Does it please the Master when even in our zeal for His work we annoy anxious friends by carelessness in little things of this kind?

May every step of our feet be more and more like those of our beloved Master. Let us continually consider Him in this, and go where He would have gone, on the errands which He would have done, "following hard" after Him. And let us look on to the time when our feet shall stand in the gates of the heavenly Jerusalem, when holy feet shall tread the streets of the holy city; no longer pacing any lonely path, for He hath said, "They shall walk with Me in white."

> "And He hath said, 'How beautiful the feet!'
> The 'feet' so weary, travel-stained, and worn—
> The 'feet' that humbly, patiently have borne
> The toilsome way, the pressure, and the heat.
>
> "The 'feet,' not hasting on with wingèd might,
> Nor strong to trample down the opposing foe;
> So lowly, and so human, they must go
> By painful steps to scale the mountain height.
>
> "Not unto all the tuneful lips are given,
> The ready tongue, the words so strong and sweet;
> Yet all may turn, with humble, willing 'feet,'
> And bear to darkened souls the light from heaven.

"And fall they while the goal far distant lies,
 With scarce a word yet spoken for their Lord—
 His sweet approval He doth yet accord;
Their 'feet' are beauteous in the Master's eyes.

"With weary human 'feet' He, day by day,
 Once trod this earth to work His acts of love;
 And every step is chronicled above
His servants take to follow in His way."

SARAH GERALDINA STOCK.

CHAPTER V.

Our Voices Kept for Jesus.

"Keep my voice, and let me sing
Always, only, for my King."

I HAVE wondered a little at being told by an experienced worker, that in many cases the voice seems the last and hardest thing to yield entirely to the King; and that many who think and say they have consecrated all to the Lord and His service, "revolt" when it comes to be a question of whether they shall sing "always, only," for their King. They do not mind singing a few general sacred songs, but they do not see their way to really singing always and only unto and for Him. They want to bargain and balance a little. They question and argue about what proportion they may keep for self-pleasing and company-pleasing, and how much they must "give up"; and who will and who won't like it; and what they "really *must* sing," and what they "really must *not* sing," at certain times and places; and what "won't do," and what they "can't very well help," and so on. And so when the question "How much owest thou unto my Lord?" is applied to this particularly pleasant gift, it is not met with the loyal, free-hearted, happy response, "All! yes, *all* for Jesus!"

I know there are special temptations around this matter. Vain and selfish ones—whispering how much better a certain song suits your voice, and how much more likely to be admired. Faithless ones—suggesting doubts whether you can make the holy song "go." Specious ones—asking whether you ought not to please your neighbours, and hushing up the rest of the precept, "Let every one of you please his neighbour *for his good to edification*" (Romans 15:2). Cowardly ones—telling you that it is just a little too much to expect of you, and that you are not called upon to wave your banner in people's very faces, and provoke surprise and remark, as this might do. And so the banner is kept furled, the witness for Jesus is not borne, and you sing for others and not for your King.

The words had passed your lips, "Take my voice!" And yet you will not let Him have it; you will not let Him have that which costs you something, just *because* it costs you something! And yet He lent you that pleasant voice that you might use it for Him. And yet He, in the sureness of His perpetual presence, was beside you all the while, and heard every note as you sang the songs which were, as your inmost heart knew, *not* for Him.

Where is your faith? Where is the consecration you have talked about? The voice has not been kept for Him, because it has not been truly and unreservedly given to Him. Will you not now say, "Take my voice, for I had not given it to Thee; keep my voice, for I cannot keep it for Thee"?

And He will keep it! You cannot tell, till you have tried, how surely all the temptations flee when it is no longer your battle but the Lord's; nor how completely and *curiously* all the difficulties vanish, when you simply and trustfully go forward in the path of full consecration in this matter. You will find that the keeping is most wonderfully real. Do not expect to lay down rules and provide for every sort of contingency. If you could, you would miss the sweetness of the continual guidance in the "kept" course. Have only one rule about it—just to look up to your Master about every single song you are asked or feel inclined to sing. If you are "willing and obedient," you will always meet His guiding eye. He will always keep the voice that is wholly at His disposal. Soon you will have such experience of His immediate guidance that you will be utterly satisfied with it, and only sorrowfully wonder you did not sooner thus simply lean on it.

I have just received a letter from one who has laid her special gift at the feet of the Giver, yielding her voice to Him with hearty desire that it might be kept for His use. She writes: "I had two lessons on singing while in Germany from our Master. One was very sweet. A young girl wrote to me, that when she had heard me sing, 'O come, every one that thirsteth,' she went away and prayed that she might come, and she *did* come, too. Is not He good? The other was: I had been tempted to join the *Gesang Verein* in N——. I prayed to be shown whether I was right in so doing or not. I did not see my way clear, so I went. The singing was all secular. The very first night I went I caught a bad cold on my chest, which prevented me from singing again at all till Christmas. Those were better than any lessons from a singing master!" Does not this illustrate both the keeping *from* and the keeping *for*? In the latter case I believe she honestly wished to know her Lord's will,—whether the training and practise were needed for His better service with her music, and that, therefore, she might take them for His sake; or whether the concomitants and influence would be such as to hinder the close communion with Him which she had found so precious, and that, therefore, she was to trust Him to give her "much more than this."

And so, at once, He showed her unmistakeably what He would have her *not* do, and gave her the sweet consciousness that He Himself was teaching her and taking her at her word. I know what her passionate love for music is, and how very real and great the compensation from Him must have been which could thus make her right down *glad* about what would otherwise have been an immense disappointment. And then, as to the former of these two "lessons," the song she names was one substituted when she said, "Take my voice," for some which were far more effective for her voice. But having freely chosen to sing what might glorify the Master rather than the singer, see how, almost immediately, He gave her a reward infinitely outweighing all the drawing-room compliments or concert-room applause! That one consecrated song found echoes in heaven, bringing, by its blessed result, joy to the angels and glory to God. And the memory of that song is immortal; it will live through ages to come, never lost, never dying away, when the vocal triumphs of the world's greatest singers are past and forgotten for ever. Now you who have been taking a half-and-half course, do you get such rewards as this? You may well envy them! But why not take the same decided course, and share the same blessed keeping and its fulness of hidden reward?

If you only knew, dear hesitating friends, what strength and gladness the Master gives when we loyally "sing forth the honour of His Name," you would not forego it! Oh, if you only knew the difficulties it saves! For when you sing "always and only for your King," you will not get much entangled by the King's enemies. Singing an out-and-out sacred song often clears one's path at a stroke as to many other things. If you only knew the rewards He gives—very often then and there; the recognition that you are one of the King's friends by some lonely and timid one; the openings which you quite naturally gain of speaking a word for Jesus to hearts which, without the song, would never have given you the chance of the word! If you only knew the joy of believing that His sure promise, "My Word shall not return unto Me void," will be fulfilled as you *sing* that word for Him! If you only tasted the solemn happiness of knowing that you have indeed a royal audience, that the King Himself is listening as you sing! If you only knew—and why should you not know? Shall not the time past of your life suffice you for the miserable, double-hearted, calculating service? Let Him have the *whole* use of your voice at any cost, and see if He does not put many a totally unexpected new song into your mouth!

I am not writing all this to great and finished singers, but to everybody who can sing at all. Those who think they have only a very small talent, are often most tempted not to trade with it for their Lord. Whether you have much or little natural voice, there is reason for its cultivation and room for its use. Place it at your Lord's disposal, and He will show you how to make the most of it for Him; for not seldom His multiplying power is brought to bear on a consecrated voice. A puzzled singing master, very famous in his profession, said to one who tried to sing for Jesus, "Well, you have not much voice; but, mark my words, you will always beat anybody with four times your voice!" He was right, though he did not in the least know why.

A great many so-called "sacred songs" are so plaintive and pathetic that they help to give a gloomy idea of religion. Now *don't* sing these; come out boldly, and sing definitely and unmistakeably for your King, and of your King, and to your King. You will soon find, and even outsiders will have to own, that it is a *good* thing thus to show forth His loving-kindness and His faithfulness (see Psalm 92:1–3).

Here I am usually met by the query, "But what would you advise me to sing?" I can only say that I never got any practical help from asking any one but the Master Himself, and so I would advise you to do the same! He knows exactly what will best suit your voice and enable you to sing best for Him; for He made it, and gave it just the pitch and tone He pleased, so, of course, He is the best counsellor about it. Refer your question in simplest faith to Him, and I am perfectly sure you will find it answered. He will direct you, and in some way or other the Lord will provide the right songs for you to sing. That is the very best advice I can possibly give you on the subject, and you will prove it to be so if you will act upon it.

Only one thing I would add: I believe there is nothing like singing His own words. The preacher claims the promise, "My Word shall not return unto Me void," and why should not the singer equally claim it? Why should we use His own inspired words, with faith in their power, when speaking or writing, and content ourselves with human words put into rhyme (and sometimes very feeble rhyme) for our singing?

What a vista of happy work opens out here! What is there to prevent our using this mightiest of all agencies committed to human agents, the Word, which is quick and powerful, and sharper than any two-edged sword, whenever we are asked to sing? By this means, even a young girl may be privileged to make that Word sound in the ears of many who would not listen to it otherwise. By this, the incorruptible seed may be sown in otherwise unreachable ground.

It is a remarkable fact that it is actually the easiest way thus to take the very highest ground. You will find that singing Bible words does not excite the prejudice or contempt that any other words, sufficiently decided to be worth singing, are almost sure to do. For very decency's sake, a Bible song will be listened to respectfully; and for very shame's sake, no adverse whisper will be ventured against the words in ordinary English homes. The singer is placed on a vantage-ground, certain that at least the words of the song will be outwardly respected, and the possible ground of unfriendly criticism thus narrowed to begin with.

But there is much more than this. One feels the power of His words for oneself as one sings. One loves them and rejoices in them, and what can be greater help to any singer than that? And one knows they are true, and that they cannot really return void, and what can give greater confidence than that? God *may* bless the singing of any words, but He *must* bless the singing of His own Word, if that promise means what it says!

The only real difficulty in the matter is that Scripture songs, as a rule, require a little more practise than others. Then practise them a little more! You think nothing of the trouble of learning, for instance, a sonata, which takes you many a good hour's practise before you can render it perfectly and expressively. But you shrink from a song, the accompaniment of which you cannot read off without any trouble at all. And you never think of such a thing as taking one-tenth the pains to learn that accompaniment that you took to learn that sonata! Very likely, too, you take the additional pains to learn the sonata off by heart, so that you may play it more effectively. But you do not take pains to learn your accompaniment by heart, so that you may throw all your power into the expression of the words, undistracted by reading the notes and turning over the leaves. It is far more useful to have half a dozen Scripture songs thoroughly learnt and made your own, than to have in your portfolios several dozen easy settings of sacred poetry which you get through with your eyes fixed on the notes. And every one thus thoroughly mastered makes it easier to master others.

You will say that all this refers only to drawing-room singing. So it does, primarily, but then it is the drawing-room singing which has been so little for Jesus and so much for self and society; and so much less has been said about it, and so much less *done*. There would not be half the complaints of the difficulty of witnessing for Christ in even professedly Christian homes and circles, if every converted singer were also a consecrated one. For nothing raises or lowers the tone of a whole evening so much as the character of the music. There are few things which show more clearly that, as a rule, a very definite step in advance is needed beyond being a believer or even a worker for Christ. Over how many grand or cottage pianos could the Irish Society's motto, "For Jesus' sake *only*," be hung, without being either a frequent reproach, or altogether inappropriate?

But what is learnt will, naturally, be sung. And oh! how many Christian parents give their daughters the advantage of singing lessons without troubling themselves in the least about what songs are learnt, provided they are not exceptionally foolish! Still more pressingly I would say, how many Christian principals, to whom young lives are entrusted at the most important time of all for training, do not give themselves the least concern about this matter! As I write, I turn aside to refer to a list of songs learnt last term by a fresh young voice which would willingly be trained for higher work. There is just one "sacred" song in the whole long list, and even that hardly such a one as the writer of the letter above quoted would care to sing in her fervent-spirited service of Christ. All the rest are harmless and pleasing, but only suggestive of the things of earth, the things of the world that is passing away; not one that might lead upward and onward, not one that might touch a careless heart to seek first the kingdom of God, not one that might show forth the glory and praise of our King, not one that tells out His grace and love, not one that carries His comfort to His weary ones or His joy to His loving ones. She is left to find and learn *such* songs as best she may; those which she will sing with all the ease and force gained by good teaching of them are no help at all, but rather hindrance in anything like wish or attempt to "sing *for Jesus*."

There is not the excuse that the songs of God's kingdom, songs which waft His own words to the souls around, would not have answered the teacher's purpose as well. God has taken care of that. He has not left Himself without witness in this direction. He has given the most perfect melodies and the richest harmonies to be linked with His own words, and no singer can be trained beyond His wonderful provision in this way. I pray that even these poor words of mine may reach the consciences of some of those who have this responsibility, and lead them to be no longer unfaithful in this important matter, no longer giving this strangely divided service—training, as they profess to desire, the souls for God, and yet allowing the voices to be trained only for the world.

But we must not run away with the idea that singing sacred songs and singing for Jesus are convertible terms. I know by sorrowful personal experience that it is very possible to sing a sacred song and *not* sing it for Jesus. It is easier to have one's portfolio all right than one's heart, and the repertory is more easily arranged than the motives. When we have taken our side, and the difficulties of indecision are consequently swept away, we have a new set of more subtle temptations to encounter. And although the Master will keep, the servant must watch and pray; and it is through the watching and the praying that the keeping will be effectual. We have, however, rather less excuse here than even elsewhere. For we never have to sing so very suddenly that we need be taken unawares. We have to think what to sing, and perhaps find the music, and the prelude has to be played, and all this gives quite enough time for us to recollect whose we are and whom we serve, and to arouse to the watch. Quite enough, too, for quick, trustful prayer that our singing may be kept free from that wretched self-seeking or even self-consciousness, and kept entirely for Jesus. Our best and happiest singing will flow when there is a sweet, silent undercurrent of prayerful or praiseful communion with our Master all through the song. As for nervousness, I am quite sure this is the best antidote to that.

On the other hand, it is quite possible to sing for Jesus without singing a sacred song. Do not take an ell[1] for the inch this seems to give, and run off with the idea that it does not matter after all what you sing, so that you sing in a good frame of mind! No such thing! And the admission needs very careful guarding, and must not be wrested into an excuse for looking back to the world's songs. But cases may and do arise in which it may be right to gratify weary father, or win a wayward brother, by trying to please them with music to which they will listen when they would not listen to the songs you would rather sing. There are cases in which this may be done most truly for the Lord's sake, and clearly under His guidance.

Sometimes cases arise in which we can only say, "Neither know we what to do, but our eyes are upon Thee." And when we honestly say that, depend upon it we shall find the promise true, "I will guide thee with Mine eye." For God is faithful, who will not suffer you to be tempted above that ye are able, but will, with the temptation, also make a way (Gr. *the* way) to escape, that ye may be able to bear it.

I do not know why it should be so, but it certainly is a much rarer thing to find a young gentleman singing for Jesus than a young lady,—a *very* rare thing to find one with a cultivated voice consecrating it to the Master's use. I have met some who were not ashamed to speak for Him, to whom it never seemed even to occur to sing for Him. They would go and teach a Bible class one day, and the next they would be practising or performing just the same songs as those who care nothing for Christ and His blood-bought salvation. They had left some things behind, but they had not left any of their old songs behind. They do not seem to think that being made new creatures in Christ Jesus had anything to do with this department of their lives. Nobody could gather whether they were on the Lord's side or not, as they stood and sang their neutral songs. The banner that was displayed in the class-room was furled in the drawing-room. Now, my friends, you who have or may have far greater opportunities of displaying that banner than we womenkind, why should you be less brave and loyal than your sisters? We are weak and you are strong naturally, but recollect that want

---

[1] An "ell" is an old measure of length, approximately 45 inches.

of decision always involves want of power, and compromising Christians are always weak Christians. You will never be mighty to the pulling down of strongholds while you have one foot in the enemy's camp, or on the supposed neutral ground, if such can exist (which I doubt), between the camps. You will never be a terror to the devil till you have enlisted every gift and faculty on the Lord's side. Here is a thing in which you may practically carry out the splendid motto, "All for Jesus." You cannot be all for Him as long as your voice is not for Him. Which shall it be? *All* for Him, or *partly* for Him? Answer that to Him whom you call Master and Lord.

When once this drawing-room question is settled, there is not much need to expatiate about other forms of singing for Jesus. As we have opportunity we shall be willing to do good with our pleasant gift in any way or place, and it is wonderful what nice opportunities He makes for us. Whether to one little sick child, or to a thousand listeners, according to the powers and openings granted, we shall take our happy position among those who minister with singing (1 Chronicles 6:32). And in so far as we really do this unto the Lord, I am quite sure He gives the hundredfold now in this present time more than all the showy songs or self-gratifying performances we may have left for His sake. As we steadily tread this part of the path of consecration, we shall find the difficulties left behind, and the real pleasantness of the way reached, and it will be a delight to say to oneself, "I *cannot* sing the old songs"; and though you have thought it quite enough to say, "With my song will I please my friends," especially if they happened to be pleased with a mildly sacred song or two, you will strike a higher and happier, a richer and purer note, and say with David, "With my song will I praise *Him*." David said also, "My lips shall greatly rejoice *when* I sing unto Thee, and my soul, which Thou hast redeemed." And you will find that this comes true.

> Singing for Jesus, our Saviour and King;
> 　Singing for Jesus, the Lord whom we love!
> All adoration we joyously bring,
> 　Longing to praise as they praise Him above.
>
> Singing for Jesus, our Master and Friend,
> 　Telling His love and His marvellous grace,—
> Love from eternity, love to the end,
> 　Love for the loveless, the sinful, and base.
>
> Singing for Jesus, and trying to win
> 　Many to love Him, and join in the song;

Calling the weary and wandering in,
  Rolling the chorus of gladness along.

Singing for Jesus, our Life and our Light;
  Singing for Him as we press to the mark;
Singing for Him when the morning is bright;
  Singing, still singing, for Him in the dark !

Singing for Jesus, our Shepherd and Guide;
  Singing for gladness of heart that He gives;
Singing for wonder and praise that He died;
  Singing for blessing and joy that He lives!

Singing for Jesus, oh, singing with joy;
  Thus will we praise Him, and tell out His love,
Till He shall call us to brighter employ,
  Singing for Jesus for ever above.

CHAPTER VI.

Our Lips Kept for Jesus.

*"Keep my lips, that they may be
Filled with messages from Thee."*

THE days are past for ever when we said, "Our lips are our own." Now we
know that they are not our own.

And yet how many of my readers often have the miserable consciousness
that they have "spoken unadvisedly with their lips"! How many pray, "Keep
the door of my lips," when the very last thing they think of expecting is that
they *will* be kept! They deliberately make up their minds that hasty words, or
foolish words, or exaggerated words, according to their respective temptations,
must and will slip out of that door, and that it can't be helped. The extent of
the real meaning of their prayer was merely that not quite so many might slip
out. As their faith went no farther, the answer went no farther, and so the door
was not kept.

Do let us look the matter straight in the face. Either we have committed our lips to our Lord, or we have not. This question must be settled first. If
not, oh, do not let another hour pass! Take them to Jesus, and ask Him to take
them.

But when you *have* committed them to Him, it comes to this,—is He able
or is He not able to keep that which you have committed to Him? If He is not
able, of course you may as well give up at once, for your own experience has
abundantly proved that *you* are not able, so there is no help for you. But if He
is able—nay, thank God there is no "*if*" on this side!—say, rather, *as* He is able,
where was this inevitable necessity of perpetual failure? You have been fancying yourself virtually doomed and fated to it, and therefore you have gone on
in it, while all the time His arm was not shortened that it could not save, but
you have been limiting the Holy One of Israel. Honestly, now, have you trusted

Him to keep your lips *this day?* Trust necessarily implies expectation that what
we have entrusted will be kept. If you have not expected Him to keep, you have
not trusted. You may have tried, and tried very hard, but you have not *trusted*,
and therefore you have not been kept, and your lips have been the snare of your
soul (Proverbs 18:7).

Once I heard a beautiful prayer which I can never forget; it was this: "Lord,
take my lips, and speak through them; take my mind, and think through it;
take my heart, and set it on fire." And this is the way the Master keeps the lips
of His servants, by so filling their hearts with His love that the outflow cannot
be unloving, by so filling their thoughts that the utterance cannot be un-Christ-
like. There must be filling before there *can* be pouring out; and if there is filling, there *must be* pouring out, for He hath said, "Out of the abundance of the
heart the mouth speaketh."

But I think we should look for something more direct and definite than
this. We are not all called to be the King's ambassadors, but *all* who have heard
the messages of salvation for themselves are called to be "the Lord's messengers,"
and day by day, as He gives us opportunity, we are to deliver "the Lord's message
unto the people." That message, as committed to Haggai, was, "I am with you,
saith the Lord." Is there not work enough for any lifetime in unfolding and dis-
tributing that one message to His own people? Then, for those who are still far
off, we have that equally full message from our Lord to give out, which He has
condensed for us into the one word, "Come!"

It is a specially sweet part of His dealings with His messengers that He always gives us the message for ourselves first. It is what He has first told us
in darkness—that is, in the secrecy of our own rooms, or at least of our own
hearts—that He bids us speak in light. And so the more we sit at His feet and
watch to see what He has to say to ourselves, the more we shall have to tell to
others. He does not send us out with sealed despatches, which we know nothing about, and with which we have no concern.

There seems a seven-fold sequence in His filling the lips of His messengers.
First, they must be purified. The live coal from off the altar must be laid upon
them, and He must say, "Lo, this hath touched thy lips, and thine iniquity is
taken away, and thy sin is purged." Then He will create the fruit of them, and
this seems to be the great message of peace, "Peace to him that is far off and to
him that is near saith the Lord; and I will heal him" (see Isaiah 57:19). Then
comes the prayer, "O Lord, open Thou my lips," and its sure fulfilment. For
then come in the promises, "Behold, I have put My words in thy mouth," and,
"They shall withal be fitted in thy lips." Then, of course, "the lips of the righteous feed many," for the food is the Lord's own giving. Everything leads up to

praise, and so we come next to "My mouth shall praise Thee with joyful lips, when I remember Thee." And lest we should fancy that "*when*" rather implies that it is not, or cannot be, exactly *always*, we find that the mediation of Jesus throws this added light upon it, "By *Him*, therefore, let us offer the sacrifice of praise to God *continually*, that is, the fruit of our lips, giving thanks to" (margin, confessing) "His name."

Does it seem a coming down from the mount to glance at one of our King's commandments, which is specially needful and applicable to this matter of our lips being kept for Him? "Watch and pray, that ye enter not into temptation." None of His commands clash with or supersede one another. Trusting does not supersede watching; it does but complete and effectuate it. Unwatchful trust is a delusion, and untrustful watching is in vain. Therefore let us not either wilfully or carelessly *enter* into temptation, whether of place, or person, or topic, which has any tendency to endanger the keeping of our lips for Jesus. Let us pray that grace may be more and more poured into our lips as it was into His so that our speech may be *alway* with grace. May they be pure, and sweet, and lovely, even as "His lips, like lilies, dropping sweet-smelling myrrh."

We can hardly consider the keeping of our lips without recollecting that upon them, more than all else (though not exclusively of all else), depends that greatest of our responsibilities, our influence. We have no choice in the matter; we cannot evade or avoid it; and there is no more possibility of our limiting it, or even tracing its limits, than there is of setting a bound to the far-vibrating sound-waves, or watching their flow through the invisible air. Not one sentence that passes these lips of ours but must be an invisibly prolonged influence, not dying away into silence, but living away into the words and deeds of others. The thought would not be quite so oppressive if we could know what we have done and shall be continuing to do by what we have said. But we *never* can, as a matter of fact. We may trace it a little way, and get a glimpse of some results for good or evil; but we never can see any more of it than we can see of a shooting star flashing through the night with a momentary revelation of one step of its strange path. Even if the next instant plunges it into apparent annihilation as it strikes the atmosphere of the earth, we know that it is not really so, but that its mysterious material and force must be added to the complicated materials and forces with which it has come in contact, with a modifying power none the less real because it is beyond our ken. And this is not comparing a great thing with a small, but a small thing with a great. For what is material force compared with moral force? what are gases, and vapours, and elements, compared with souls and the eternity for which they are preparing?

We all know that there is influence exerted by a person's mere presence, without the utterance of a single word. We are conscious of this every day. People seem to carry an atmosphere with them, which *must* be breathed by those whom they approach. Some carry an atmosphere in which all unkind thoughts shrivel up and cannot grow into expression. Others carry one in which "thoughts of Christ and things divine" never seem able to flourish. Have you not felt how a happy conversation about the things we love best is checked, or even strangled, by the entrance of one who is not in sympathy? Outsiders have not a chance of ever really knowing what delightful intercourse we have one with another about these things, because their very presence chills and changes it. On the other hand, how another person's incoming freshens and develops it and warms us all up, and seems to give us, without the least conscious effort, a sort of *lift!*

If even unconscious and involuntary influence is such a power, how much greater must it be when the recognised power of words is added!

It has often struck me as a matter of observation, that open profession adds force to this influence, on whichever side it weighs; and also that it has the effect of making many a word and act, which might in other hands have been as nearly neutral as anything can be, tell with by no means neutral tendency on the wrong side. The question of Eliphaz comes with great force when applied to one who desires or professes to be consecrated altogether, life *and* lips: "Should *he* reason with unprofitable talk, and with speeches *wherewith one can do no good?*" There is our standard! Idle words, which might have fallen comparatively harmlessly from one who had never named the Name of Christ, may be a stumbling-block to inquirers, a sanction to thoughtless juniors, and a grief to thoughtful seniors, when they come from lips which are professing to feed many. Even intelligent talk on general subjects by such a one may be a chilling disappointment to some craving heart, which had indulged the hope of getting help, comfort, or instruction in the things of God by listening to the conversation. It may be a lost opportunity of giving and gaining no one knows *how* much!

How well I recollect this disappointment to myself, again and again, when a mere child! In those early seeking days I never could understand why, sometimes, a good man whom I heard preach or speak as if he loved Christ very much, talked about all sorts of other things when we came back from church or missionary meeting. I did so wish he would have talked about the Saviour, whom I wanted, but had not found. It would have been so much more interesting even to the apparently thoughtless and merry little girl. How could he help it, I wondered, if he cared for that Pearl of Great Price as I was sure I should care for it if I could only find it! And oh, why didn't they ever talk to me about it, instead of about my lessons or their little girls at home? They did not know how their conversation was observed and compared with their sermon or speech, and how a hungry little soul went empty away from the supper table.

The lips of younger Christians may cause, in their turn, no less disappointment. One sorrowful lesson I can never forget; and I will tell the story in hope that it may save others from causes of similar regret. During a summer visit just after I had left school, a class of girls about my own age came to me a few times for an hour's singing. It was very pleasant indeed, and the girls were delighted with the hymns. They listened to all I had to say about time and expression, and not with less attention to the more shyly-ventured remarks about the words. Sometimes I accompanied them afterwards down the avenue; and whenever I met any of them I had smiles and plenty of kindly words for each, which they seemed to appreciate immensely. A few years afterwards I sat by the bedside of one of these girls—the most gifted of them all with both heart and head. She had been led by a wonderful way, and through long and deep suffering, into far clearer light than I enjoyed, and had witnessed for Christ in more ways than one, and far more brightly than I had ever done. She told me how sorrowfully and eagerly she was seeking Jesus at the time of those singing classes. And I never knew it, because I never asked, and she was too shy to speak first! But she told me more, and every word was a pang to me,—how she used to linger in the avenue on those summer evenings, longing that I would speak to her about the Saviour; how she hoped, week after week, that I would just stretch out a hand to help her, just say one little word that might be God's message of peace to her, instead of the pleasant, general remarks about the nice hymns and tunes. And I never did! And she went on for months, I think for years, after, without the light and gladness which it might have been my privilege to bring to her life. God chose other means, for the souls that He has given to Christ cannot be lost because of the unfaithfulness of a human instrument. But she said, and the words often ring in my ears when I am tempted to let an opportunity slip, "Ah, Miss F., I ought to have been *yours!*"

Yes, it is true enough that we should show forth His praise not only with our lips, but in our lives; but with very many Christians the other side of the prayer wants praying—they want rousing up even to *wish* to show it forth not only in their lives but with their lips. I wonder how many, even of those who read this, really pray, "O Lord, open Thou *my* lips, and my mouth shall show forth Thy praise."

And when opened, oh, how much one *does* want to have them so kept for Jesus that He may be free to make the most of them, not letting them render second-rate and indirect service when they might be doing direct and first-rate service to His cause and kingdom! It is terrible how much less is done for Him than *might* be done, in consequence of the specious notion that if what we are doing or saying is not bad, we are doing good in a certain way, and therefore may be quite easy about it. We should think a man rather foolish if he went on doing work which earned five shillings a week, when he might just as well do work in the same establishment and under the same master which would bring him in five pounds a week. But we should pronounce him shamefully dishonest and dishonourable if he accepted such handsome wages as the five pounds, and yet chose to do work worth only five shillings, excusing himself by saying that it was work all the same, and somebody had better do it. Do we not act something like this when we take the lower standard, and spend our strength in just making ourselves agreeable and pleasant, creating a general good impression in favour of religion, showing that we can be all things to all men, and that one who is supposed to be a citizen of the other world can be very well up in all that concerns this world? This may be good, but is there nothing better? What does it profit if we do make this favourable impression on an outsider, if we go no farther and do not use the influence gained to bring him right inside the fold, inside the only ark of safety? People are not converted by this sort of work; at any rate, *I* never met or heard of any one. "He thinks it better for his quiet influence to tell!" said an affectionately excusing relative of one who had plenty of special opportunities of soul-winning, if he had only used his lips as well as his life for his Master. "And how many souls have been converted to God by his 'quiet influence' all these years?" was my reply. And to that there was no answer! For the silent shining was all very beautiful in theory, but not one of the many souls placed specially under his influence had been known to be brought out of darkness into marvellous light. If they had, they must have been known, for such light can't help being seen.

When one has even a glimmer of the tremendous difference between having Christ and being without Christ; when one gets but one shuddering glimpse of what eternity is, and of what it must mean, as well as what it may mean, without Christ; when one gets but a flash of realization of the tremendous fact that all these neighbours of ours, rich and poor alike, will *have* to spend that eternity either with Him or without Him,—it is hard, very hard indeed, to understand how a man or woman can believe these things at all, and make no effort for anything beyond the temporal elevation of those around, sometimes not even beyond their amusements! "People must have entertainment," they urge. I do not find that *must* in the Bible, but I do find, "We *must* all stand before the judgment-seat of Christ." And if you have any sort of belief in that, how can you care to use those lips of yours, which might be a fountain of life to the dying

souls before you, merely to "entertain" them at your penny reading or other entertainment? As you sow, so you reap. The amusing paper is read, or the lively
ballad recited, or the popular song sung, and you reap your harvest of laughter
or applause, and of complacence at your success in "entertaining" the people.
And there it ends, when you might have sown words from which you and they
should reap fruit unto life eternal. Is this worthy work for one who has been
bought with such a price that he must say,

> "Love so amazing, so divine,
> Demands my soul, my life, my all"?

So far from yielding "all" to that rightful demand of amazing love, he does
not even yield the fruit of his lips to it, much less the lips themselves. I cannot
refrain from adding, that even this lower aim of "entertaining" is by no means
so appreciated as is supposed. As a cottager of no more than average sense and
intelligence remarked, "It was all so *trifling* at the reading; I wish gentlefolks
would believe that poor people like something better than what's just to make
them laugh." After all, nothing really pays like direct, straightforward, uncom-
promising words about God and His works and Word. Nothing else ever made
a man say, as a poor Irishman did when he heard the Good News for the first
time, "Thank ye, sir; you've taken the hunger off us to-day!"

Jephthah uttered all his words before the Lord; what about ours? Well,
they are all uttered before the Lord in one sense, whether we will or no; for
there is not a word in my tongue, but lo, Thou, O Lord, knowest it altogether!
How solemn is this thought, but how sweet does it become when our words
are uttered consciously before the Lord as we walk in the light of His perpetual
presence! Oh that we may so walk, that we may so speak, with kept feet and
kept lips, trustfully praying, "Let the meditation of my heart and the words
of my mouth be alway acceptable in Thy sight, O Lord, my Strength and my
Redeemer!"

Bearing in mind that it is not only the words which pass their lightly-hinged
portal, but our literal lips which are to be kept for Jesus, it cannot be out of
place, before closing this chapter, to suggest that they open both ways. What
passes in should surely be considered as well as what passes out. And very many
of us are beginning to see that the command, "Whether ye eat or drink, or
whatsoever ye do, do all to the glory of God," is not fully obeyed when we drink,
merely because we like it, what is the very greatest obstacle to that glory in this
realm of England. What matter that we prefer taking it in a more refined form,

if the thing itself is daily and actively and mightily working misery, and crime, and death, and destruction to thousands, till the cry thereof seems as if it must pierce the very heavens! And so it does—sooner, a great deal, than it pierces the walls of our comfortable dining-room! I only say here, you who have said, "Take my lips," stop and repeat that prayer next time you put that to your lips which is binding men and women hand and foot, and delivering them over, helpless, to Satan! Let those words pass once more from your heart *out* through your lips, and I do not think you will feel comfortable in letting the means of such infernal work pass *in* through them.

CHAPTER VII.

Our Silver and Gold Kept for Jesus.

"Keep my silver and my gold;
Not a mite would I withhold."

"THE silver and the gold is Mine, saith the Lord of Hosts." Yes, every coin we have is literally our "Lord's money." Simple belief of this fact is the stepping-stone to full consecration of what He has given us, whether much or little.

"Then you mean to say we are never to spend anything on ourselves?" Not so. Another fact must be considered,—the fact that our Lord has given us our bodies as a special personal charge, and that we are responsible for keeping these bodies, according to the means given and the work required, in working order for Him. This is part of our "own work." A master entrusts a workman with a delicate machine, with which his appointed work is to be done. He also provides him with a sum of money with which he is to procure all that may be necessary for keeping the machine in thorough repair. Is it not obvious that it is the man's distinct duty to see to this faithfully? Would he not be failing in duty if he chose to spend it all on something for somebody else's work, or on a present for his master, fancying that would please him better, while the machine is creaking and wearing for want of a little oil, or working badly for want of a new band or screw? Just so, we are to spend what is really needful *on* ourselves, because it is our charge to do so; but not *for* ourselves, because we are not our own, but our Master's. He who knoweth our frame, knows its need of rest and medicine, food and clothing; and the procuring of these for our own entrusted bodies should be done just as much "for Jesus" as the greater pleasure of procuring them for some one else. Therefore there need be no quibbling over the assertion that consecration is not real and complete while we are looking upon a single shilling as our own to do what we like with. Also the principle is exactly the same, whether we are spending pence or pounds; it is our Lord's money, and must not be spent without reference to Him.

When we have asked Him to take, and continually trust Him to keep our money, "shopping" becomes a different thing. We look up to our Lord for guidance to lay out His money prudently and rightly, and as He would have us lay it out. The gift or garment is selected consciously under His eye, and with conscious reference to Him as our own dear Master, for whose sake we shall give it, or in whose service we shall wear it, and whose own silver or gold we shall pay for it, and then it is all right.

But have you found out that it is one of the secrets of the Lord, that when any of His dear children turn aside a little bit after having once entered the blessed path of true and conscious consecration, He is sure to send them some little punishment? He will not let us go back without a sharp, even if quite secret, reminder. Go and spend ever such a little without reference to Him after you have once pledged the silver and gold entirely to Him, and see if you are not in some way rebuked for it! Very often by being permitted to find that you have made a mistake in your purchase, or that in some way it does not prosper. If you "observe these things," you will find that the more closely we are walking with our Lord, the more immediate and unmistakeable will be His gracious rebukes when we swerve in any detail of the full consecration to which He has called us. And if you have already experienced and recognised this part of His personal dealing with us, you will know also how we love and bless Him for it.

There is always a danger that just because we say "all," we may practically fall shorter than if we had only said "some," but said it very definitely. God recognises this, and provides against it in many departments. For instance, though our time is to be "all" for Him, yet He solemnly sets apart the one day in seven which is to be specially for Him. Those who think they know better than God, and profess that every day is a Sabbath, little know what floodgates of temptation they are opening by being so very wise above what is written. God knows best, and that should be quite enough for every loyal heart. So, as to money, though we place it all at our Lord's disposal, and rejoice to spend it all for Him directly or indirectly, yet I am quite certain it is a great help and safeguard, and, what is more, a matter of simple obedience to the spirit of His commands, to set aside a definite and regular proportion of our income or receipts for His direct service. It is a great mistake to suppose that the law of giving the tenth to God is merely Levitical. "Search and look" for yourselves, and you will find that it is, like the Sabbath, a far older rule, running all through the Bible,[1] and endorsed, not abrogated, by Christ Himself. For, speaking of tithes, He said, "These *ought* ye to have done, and not to leave the other undone." To dedicate the tenth of whatever we have is mere duty; charity begins beyond it; free-will offerings and thank-offerings beyond that again.

First-fruits, also, should be thus specially set apart. This, too, we find running all through the Bible. There is a tacit appeal to our gratitude in the suggestion of them,—the very word implies bounty received and bounty in prospect. Bringing " the first of the first-fruits into the house of the Lord thy God," was like " saying grace " for all the plenty He was going to bestow on the faithful Israelite. Something of gladness, too, seems always implied. " The day of the first-fruits " was to be a day of rejoicing (compare Numbers 28:26 with Deuteronomy 16:10, 11). There is also an appeal to loyalty: we are commanded to *honour* the Lord with the first-fruits of all our increase. And *that* is the way to prosper, for the next word is, "*So* shall thy barns be filled with plenty." The friend who first called my attention to this command, said that the setting apart first-fruits— making a proportion for God's work a *first charge* upon the income—always seemed to bring a blessing on the rest, and that since this had been systematically done, it actually seemed to go farther than when not thus lessened.

Presenting our first-fruits should be a peculiarly delightful act, as they are themselves the emblem of our consecrated relationship to God. For of His own will begat He us by the word of truth, that we should be a kind of first-fruits of His creatures. How sweet and hallowed and richly emblematic our little acts of obedience in this matter become, when we throw this light upon them! And how blessedly they may remind us of the heavenly company, singing, as it were, a new song before the throne; for they are the first-fruits unto God and to the Lamb.

Perhaps we shall find no better plan of detailed and systematic setting apart than the New Testament one: " Upon the first day of the week let every one of you lay by him in store, as God hath prospered him." The very act of literally fulfilling this apostolic command seems to bring a blessing with it, as all simple obedience does. I wish, dear friends, you would try it! You will find it a sweet reminder on His own day of this part of your consecration. You will find it an immense help in making the most of your little charities. The regular inflow

---

[1] See Genesis 14:20, 28:22; Leviticus 27:30, 32; Numbers 18:21; Deuteronomy 14:22; 2 Chronicles 31:5, 6, 12; Nehemiah 10:37, 12:44, 13:12; Malachi 3:8, 10; Matthew 23:23; Luke 11:42; 1 Corinthians 16:2; Hebrews 7:8.

will guide the outflow, and ensure your always having *something* for any sudden call for your Master's poor or your Master's cause. Do not say you are "afraid you could not keep to it." What has a consecrated life to do with being "afraid"? Some of us could tell of such sweet and singular lessons of trust in this matter, that they are written in golden letters of love on our memories. Of course there will be trials of our faith in this, as well as in everything else. But every trial of our faith is but a trial of His faithfulness, and is "much more precious than gold which perisheth."

"What about self-denial?" some reader will say. Consecration does not supersede this, but transfigures it. Literally, a consecrated life is and must be a life of denial of self. But all the effort and pain of it is changed into very delight. We love our Master; we know, surely and absolutely, that He is listening and watching our every word and way, and that He has called us to the privilege of walking "worthy of the Lord unto all pleasing." And in so far as this is a reality to us, the identical things which are still self-*denial* in one sense, become actual self-*delight* in another. It may be self-denial to us to turn away from something within reach of our purse which it would be very convenient or pleasant to possess. But if the Master lifted the veil, and revealed Himself standing at our side, and let us hear His audible voice asking us to reserve the price of it for His treasury, should we talk about self-denial then? Should we not be utterly ashamed to think of it? or rather, should we, for one instant, think about self or self-denial at all? Would it not be an unimaginable joy to do what He asked us to do with that money? But as long as His own unchangeable promise stands written in His word for us, "Lo, I am with you *alway*," we may be sure that He *is* with us, and that His eye is as certainly on our opened or half-opened purse as it was on the treasury, when He sat over against it and saw the two mites cast in. So let us do our shopping "as seeing Him who is invisible."

It is important to remember that there is no much or little in God's sight, except as relatively to our means and willingness. "For if there be first a willing mind, it is accepted according to that a man hath, and not according to that he hath not." He knows what we have *not*, as well as what we have. He knows all about the low wages in one sphere, and the small allowance, or the fixed income with rising prices in another. And it is not a question of paying to God what can be screwed out of these, but of giving Him all, and then holding all at His disposal, and taking His orders about the disposal of all.

But I do not see at all how self-indulgence and needless extravagance can possibly co-exist with true consecration. If we really never do *go without* anything for the Lord's sake, but, just because He has graciously given us means always supply for ourselves not only every need but "every notion," I think it is high time we looked into the matter before God. Why should only those who have limited means have the privilege of offering to their Lord that which has really cost them something to offer? Observe, it is not *merely* going without something we would naturally like to have or do, but going without it *for Jesus' sake.* Not, "I will go without it, because, after all, I can't very well afford it"; or, "because I really ought to subscribe to so and so"; or, "because I daresay I shall be glad I have not spent the money:" but, "I will do without it, because I *do* want to do a little more for Him who so loves me—just that much more than I could do if I did this other thing." I fancy this is more often the heart language of those who *have* to cut and contrive, than of those who are able to give liberally without any cutting and contriving at all. The very abundance of God's good gifts too often hinders from the privilege and delight of really doing without something superfluous or comfortable or usual, that they may give just that much more to their Lord. What a pity!

The following quotation may (I hope it will) touch some conscience:—"A gentleman once told us that his wine bill was £100 a year—more than enough to keep a Scripture reader always at work in some populous district. And it is one of the countless advantages of total abstinence that it at once sets free a certain amount of money for such work. Smoking, too, is a habit not only injurious to the health in a vast majority of cases, and, to our mind, very unbecoming in a 'temple of the Holy Ghost,' but also one which squanders money which might be used for the Lord. Expenses in dress might in most people be curtailed; expensive tastes should be denied; and simplicity in all habits of life should be a mark of the followers of Him who had not where to lay His head."

And again: "The self-indulgence of wealthy Christians, who might largely support the Lord's work with what they lavish upon their houses, their tables, or their personal expenditure, is very sad to see." [1]

Here the question of jewellery seems to come in. Perhaps it was an instance of the gradual showing of the details of consecration, illustrated on page 27,[2] but I will confess that when I wrote, "Take my silver and my gold," it never dawned on me that anything was included beyond the coin of the realm! But the Lord "leads on softly," and a good many of us have been shown some capital bits of unenclosed but easily enclosable ground, which have yielded "pleasant fruit." Yes, *very* pleasant fruit! It is wonderfully nice to light upon something that we really never thought of as a possible gift to our Lord, and just to give it, straight away, to Him. I do not press the matter, but I do ask my lady friends to give it fair and candid and prayerful consideration. Which do you really care most

[1] *Christian Progress*, vol. 3. pp. 25, 26.　　[2] See page 14 of this book.

about—a diamond on your finger, or a star in the Redeemer's kingdom, shining for ever and ever? That is what it comes to, and there I leave it.

On the other hand, it is very possible to be fairly faithful in much, and yet unfaithful in that which is least. We may have thought about our gold and silver, and yet have been altogether thoughtless about out rubbish! Some have a habit of hoarding away old garments, "pieces," remnants, and odds and ends generally, under the idea that they "will come in useful some day"; very likely setting it up as a kind of mild virtue, backed by that noxious old saying, "Keep it by you seven years, and you'll find a use for it." And so the shabby things get shabbier, and moth and dust doth corrupt, and the drawers and places get choked and crowded, and meanwhile all this that is sheer rubbish to you might be made useful at once, to a degree beyond what you would guess, to some poor person.

It would be a nice variety for the clever fingers of a lady's maid to be set to work to do up old things; or some tidy woman may be found in almost every locality who knows how to contrive children's things out of what seems to you only fit for the rag-bag, either for her own little ones or those of her neighbours.

My sister trimmed 70 or 80 hats every spring for several years with the contents of friends' rubbish drawers, thus relieving dozens of poor mothers who liked their children to "go tidy on Sunday," and also keeping down finery in her Sunday school. Those who literally fulfilled her request for "rubbish" used to marvel at the results.

Little scraps of carpet, torn old curtains, faded blinds, and all such gear, go a wonderfully long way towards making poor cottagers and old or sick people comfortable. I never saw anything in this "rubbish" line yet that could not be turned to good account somehow, with a little *considering* of the poor and their discomforts.

I wish my lady reader would just leave this book now, and go straight upstairs and have a good rummage at once, and see what can be thus cleared out. If she does not know the right recipients at first hand, let her send it off to the nearest working clergyman's wife, and see how gratefully it will be received! For it is a great trial to workers among the poor not to be able to supply the needs they see. Such supplies are far more useful than treble their small money value.

Just a word of earnest pleading for needs, closely veiled, but very sore, which might be wonderfully lightened if this wardrobe overhauling were systematic and faithful. There are hundreds of poor clergymen's families to whom a few old garments or any household oddments are as great a charity as to any of the poor under their charge. There are two Societies for aiding these with such gifts, under initials which are explained in the Reports: the P.P.C. Society—Secretary, Miss Breay, Battenhall Place, Worcester; and the A.F.D. Society—Secretary, Miss Hinton, 4 York Place, Clifton. I only ask my lady friends to send for a report to either of these devoted secretaries; and if their hearts are not so touched by the cases of brave and bitter need that they go forthwith to wardrobes and drawers to see what can be spared and sent, they are colder and harder than I give English-women credit for.

There is no bondage in consecration. The two things are opposites, and cannot co-exist, much less mingle. We should suspect our consecration, and come afresh to our great Counsellor about it, directly we have any sense of bondage. As long as we have an unacknowledged feeling of fidget about our account-book, and a smothered wondering what and how much we "*ought*" to give, and a hushed-up wishing the thing had not been put quite so strongly before us, depend upon it we have not said unreservedly, "Take my silver and my gold." And how can the Lord keep what He has not been sincerely asked to take?

Ah! if we had stood at the foot of the Cross, and watched the tremendous payment of our redemption with the precious blood of Christ,—if we had seen that awful price told out, drop by drop, from His own dear patient brow and torn hands and feet, till it was ALL paid, and the central word of eternity was uttered, "*It is finished!*" should we not have been ready to say, "*Not a mite will I withhold!*"

My Jewels.

"Shall I hold them back—my jewels?
 Time has travelled many a day
Since I laid them by for ever,
 Safely locking them away;
And I thought them yielded wholly,
 When I dared no longer wear
Gems contrasting, oh, so sadly!
 With the adorning I would bear.

"Shall I keep them still—my jewels?
 Shall I, can I yet withhold
From that living, loving Saviour
 Aught of silver or of gold?

Gold so needed, that His gospel
  May resound from sea to sea;
Can I know Christ's service lacketh,
  Yet forget His 'unto Me'!

"No; I lay them down—my jewels,
  Truly on the altar now.
Stay! I see a vision passing
  Of a gem-encircled brow:
Heavenly treasure worn by Jesus,
  Souls won through my gift outpoured;
Freely, gladly I will offer
  Jewels thus to crown my Lord!"

—From *Woman's Work*.

CHAPTER VIII.

Our Intellects Kept for Jesus.

*"Keep my intellect, and use
Every power as Thou shalt choose."*

THERE are two distinct sets of temptations which assail those who have, or think they have, rather less, and those who have, or think they have, rather more than an average share of intellect; while those who have neither less nor more are generally open in some degree to both. The refuge and very present help from both is the same. The intellect, whether great or small, which is committed to the Lord's keeping, will be kept and will be used by Him.

The former class are tempted to think themselves excused from effort to cultivate and use their small intellectual gifts; to suppose they cannot or need not seek to win souls, because they are not so clever and apt in speech as So-and-so; to attribute to want of gift what is really want of grace; to hide the one talent because it is not five. Let me throw out a thought or two for these.

Which is greatest, gifts or grace? *Gifts* are given "to every man according to his several ability." That is, we have just as much given as God knows we are able to use, and what He knows we can best use for Him. "But unto every one of us is given *grace* according to the measure of the gift of Christ." Claiming and using that royal measure of grace, you may, and can, and will do more for God than the mightiest intellect in the world without it. For which, in the clear light of His Word, is likely to be most effectual, the natural ability which at its best and fullest, without Christ, "can do *nothing*" (observe and believe that word!), or the grace of our Almighty God and the power of the Holy Ghost, which is as free to you as it ever was to any one?

If you are responsible for making use of your limited gift, are you not equally responsible for making use of the grace and power which are to be had for the asking, which are already yours in Christ, and which are not limited?

Also, do you not see that where there are great natural gifts, people give the credit to *them*, instead of to the grace which alone did the real work, and thus God is defrauded of the glory? So that, to say it reverently, God can get more glory out of a feeble instrument, because then it is more obvious that the excellency of the power is of God and not of us. Will you not henceforth say, "Most gladly, therefore, will I rather glory in my infirmities, that the power of Christ may rest upon me"?

Don't you really believe that the Holy Spirit is just as able to draw a soul to Jesus, if He will, by your whisper of the one word "*Come,*" as by an eloquent sermon an hour long? *I* do! At the same time, as it is evidently God's way to work through these intellects of ours, we have no more right to expect Him to use a mind which we are wilfully neglecting, and taking no pains whatever to fit for His use, than I should have to expect you to write a beautiful inscription with my pen, if I would not take the trouble to wipe it and mend it.

The latter class are tempted to rely on their natural gifts, and to act and speak in their own strength; to go on too fast, without really looking up at every step, and for every word; to spend their Lord's time in polishing up their intellects, nominally for the sake of influence and power, and so forth, while really, down at the bottom, it is for the sake of the keen enjoyment of the process; and perhaps, most of all, to spend the strength of these intellects "for that which doth not profit," in yielding to the specious snare of reading clever books "on both sides," and eating deliberately of the tree of the knowledge of good *and evil.*

The mere mention of these temptations should be sufficient appeal to conscience. If consecration is to be a reality anywhere, should it not be in the very thing which you own as an extra gift from God, and which is evidently closest, so to speak, to His direct action, spirit upon spirit? And if the very strength of your intellect has been your weakness, will you not entreat Him to keep it henceforth really and entirely for Himself? It is so good of Him to have given you something to lay at His feet; shall not this goodness lead you to lay it *all* there, and never hanker after taking it back for yourself or the world? Do you not feel that in very proportion to the gift you need the special keeping of it? He may lead you by a way you know not in the matter; very likely He will show you that you must be willing to be a fool for His sake first, before He will condescend to use you much for His glory. Will you look up into His face and say, "*Not* willing"?

He who made every power can use every power—memory, judgment, imagination, quickness of apprehension or insight; specialties of musical, poetical, oratorical, or artistic faculty; special tastes for reasoning, philosophy, history, natural science, or natural history,—all these may be dedicated to Him, sanctified by Him, and used by Him. Whatever He has given, He will use if we will let Him. Often, in the most unexpected ways, and at the most unexpected turns, something read or acquired long ago suddenly comes into use. We cannot foresee what will thus "come in useful"; but He knew, when He guided us to learn it, what it would be wanted for in His service. So may we not ask Him to bring His perfect foreknowledge to bear on all our mental training and storing? to guide us to read or study exactly what He knows there will be use for in the work to which He has called or will call us?

Nothing is more practically perplexing to a young Christian, whose preparation time is not quite over, or perhaps painfully limited, than to know what is most worth studying, what is really the best investment of the golden hours, while yet the time is not come for the field of active work to be fully entered, and the "thoroughly furnishing" of the mind is the evident path of present duty. Is not His name called "Counsellor"? and will He not be faithful to the promise of His name in this, as well as in all else?

The same applies to every subsequent stage. Only let us be perfectly clear about the principle that our intellect is not our own, either to cultivate, or to use, or to enjoy, and that Jesus Christ is our real and ever-present Counsellor, and then there will be no more worry about what to read and how much to read, and whether to keep up one's accomplishments, or one's languages, or one's "ologies"! If the Master has need of them, He will show us; and if He has not, what need have we of them? If we go forward without His leading, we may throw away some talent, or let it get too rusty for use, which would have been most valuable when other circumstances arose or different work was given. We must not think that "keeping" means not using at all! What we want is to have all our powers kept for His *use*.

In this they will probably find far higher development than in any other sort of use. I know cases in which the effect of real consecration on mere mental development has been obvious and surprising to all around. Yet it is only a confirmation of what I believe to be a great principle, viz. that *the Lord makes the most of whatever is unreservedly surrendered to Him.* There will always be plenty of waste in what we try to cut out for ourselves. But He wastes no material!

CHAPTER IX.

Our Wills Kept for Jesus.

"Keep my will, oh, keep it Thine,
For it is no longer mine."

PERHAPS there is no point in which expectation has been so limited by experience as this. We believe God is able to do for us just so much as He has already done, and no more. We take it for granted a line must be drawn somewhere; and so we choose to draw it where experience ends, and faith would have to begin. Even if we have trusted and proved Him as to keeping our members and our minds, faith fails when we would go deeper and say, "Keep my will!" And yet the only reason we have to give is, that though we have asked Him to take our will, we do not exactly find that it is altogether His, but that self-will crops up again and again. And whatever flaw there might be in this argument, we think the matter is quite settled by the fact that some whom we rightly esteem, and who are far better than ourselves, have the same experience, and do not even seem to think it right to hope for anything better. That is conclusive! And the result of this, as of every other faithless conclusion, is either discouragement and depression, or, still worse, acquiescence in an unyielded will, as something that can't be helped.

Now let us turn from our thoughts to God's thoughts. Verily, they are not as ours! He says He is able to do exceeding abundantly above all that we ask or think. Apply this here. We ask Him to take our wills and make them His. Does He or does He not mean what He says? and if He does, should we not trust Him to do this thing that we have asked and longed for, and not less but more? "Is *anything* too hard for the Lord?" "Hath He said, and shall He not do it?" and if He gives us faith to believe that we have the petition that we desired of Him, and with it the unspeakable rest of leaning our will wholly upon His love, what ground have we for imagining that this is *necessarily* to be a mere fleeting shadow, which is hardly to last an hour, but is *necessarily* to be exhausted ere the next breath of trial or temptation comes? Does He mock our longing by acting as I have seen an older person act to a child, by accepting some trifling gift of no intrinsic value, just to please the little one, and then throwing it away as soon as the child's attention is diverted? Is not the taking rather the pledge of the keeping, if we will but entrust Him fearlessly with it? We give Him no opportunity, so to speak, of proving His faithfulness to this great promise, because we will not fulfil the condition of reception, believing it. But we readily enough believe instead all that we hear of the unsatisfactory experience of others! Or, start from another word. Job said, "I know that Thou canst do everything," and we turn round and say, "Oh yes, everything *except* keeping my will!" Dare we add, "And I know that Thou canst not do that"? Yet that is what is said every day, only in other words; and if not said aloud, it is said in faithless hearts, and God hears it. What *does* "Almighty" mean, if it does not mean, as we teach our little children, "able to do *everything*"?

We have asked this great thing many a time, without, perhaps, realizing how great a petition we were singing, in the old morning hymn, "Guard my first springs of thought and will!" That goes to the root of the matter, only it implies that the will has been already surrendered to Him, that it may be wholly kept and guarded.

It may be that we have not sufficiently realized the sin of the only alternative. Our wills belong either to self or to God. It may seem a small and rather excusable sin in man's sight to be self-willed, but see in what a category of iniquity God puts it! (2 Peter 2:10.) And certainly we are without excuse when we have such a promise to go upon as, "It is God that worketh in you both to *will* and to do of His pleasure." How splendidly this meets our very deepest helplessness,—"worketh in you to *will!*" Oh, let us pray for ourselves and for each other, that we may know "what is the exceeding greatness of His power to usward who believe." It does not say, "to usward who fear and doubt"; for if we will not believe, neither shall we be established. If we will not believe what God says He can do, we shall see it with our eyes, but we shall not eat thereof. "They *could* not enter in because of unbelief."

It is most comforting to remember that the grand promise, "Thy people shall be willing in the day of Thy power," is made by the Father to Christ Himself. The Lord Jesus holds this promise, and God will fulfil it to Him. He will make us willing because He has promised Jesus that He will do so. And what is being made willing, but having our will taken and kept?

All true surrender of the will is based upon love and knowledge of, and confidence in, the one to whom it is surrendered. We have the human analogy so often before our eyes, that it is the more strange we should be so slow to own even the possibility of it as to God. Is it thought anything so very extraordinary and high-flown, when a bride deliberately *prefers* wearing a colour which was not her own taste or choice, because her husband likes to see her in it? Is it very unnatural that it is no distress to her to do what he asks her to do, or to go with him where he asks her to come, even without question or explanation, instead of doing what or going where she would undoubtedly have preferred if she did not know and love him? Is it very surprising if this lasts beyond the wedding day, and if year after year she still finds it her greatest pleasure to please him, quite irrespective of what *used* to be her own ways and likings? Yet in this case she is not helped by any promise or power on his part to make her wish what he wishes. But He who so wonderfully condescends to call Himself the Bridegroom of His church, and who claims our fullest love and trust, has promised and has power to work in us to will. Shall we not claim His promise and rely on His mighty power, and say, not self-confidently, but looking only unto Jesus—

> "Keep my will, for it is Thine;
> It shall be no longer mine!"

Only in proportion as our own will is surrendered, are we able to discern the splendour of God's will.

> For oh! it is a splendour,
> A glow of majesty,
> A mystery of beauty,
> If we will only see;
> A very cloud of glory
> Enfolding you and me.
>
> A splendour that is lighted
> At one transcendent flame,
> The wondrous Love, the perfect Love,
> Our Father's sweetest name;
> For His Name and very Essence
> And His Will are all the same!

Conversely, in proportion as we see this splendour of His will, we shall more readily or more fully surrender our own. Not until we have presented our bodies a living sacrifice can we prove what is that good, and perfect, and acceptable will of God. But in thus proving it, this continual presentation will be more and more seen to be our reasonable service, and becomes more and more a joyful sacrifice of praise.

The connection in Romans 12:1, 2, between our sacrifice which He so graciously calls acceptable to Himself, and our finding out that His Will is acceptable to ourselves, is very striking. One reason for this connection may be that only love can really understand love, and love on both sides is at the bottom of the whole transaction and its results. First, He loves us. Then the discovery of this leads us to love Him. Then, because He loves us, He claims us, and desires to have us wholly yielded to His will, so that the operations of love in and for us may find no hindrance. Then, because we love Him we recognise His claim and yield ourselves. Then, being thus yielded, He draws us nearer to Him,[1] and admits us, so to speak, into closer intimacy, so that we gain nearer and truer views of His perfections. Then the unity of these perfections becomes clearer to us. Now we not only see His justice and mercy flowing in undivided stream from the cross of Christ, but we see that they never were divided, though the strange distortions of the dark, false glass of sin made them appear so, but that both are but emanations of God's holy love. Then having known and believed this holy love, we see further that His will is not a separate thing, but only love (and therefore all His attributes) in action; love being the primary essence of His being, and all the other attributes manifestations and combinations of that ineffable essence, for God *is* Love. Then this will of God which has seemed in old far-off days a stern and fateful power, is seen to be only love energized; love saying, "I will." And when once we really grasp this (hardly so much by faith as by love itself), the will of God cannot be otherwise than acceptable, for it is no longer a question of trusting that somehow or other there is a hidden element of love in it, but of understanding that it *is* love; no more to be dissociated from it than the power of the sun's rays can be dissociated from their light and warmth. And love recognised must surely be love accepted and reciprocated. So, as the fancied sternness of God's will is lost in His love, the stubbornness of our will becomes melted in that love, and lost in our acceptance of it.

---

[1] "Now ye *have* consecrated yourselves unto the Lord, come *near*" (2 Chronicles 29:31).

"Take Thine own way with me, dear Lord,
    Thou canst not otherwise than bless;
I launch me forth upon a sea
    Of boundless love and tenderness.

"I could not choose a larger bliss
    Than to be wholly Thine; and mine
A will whose highest joy is this,
    To ceaselessly unclasp in Thine.

"I will not fear Thee, O my God!
    The days to come can only bring
Their perfect sequences of love,
    Thy larger, deeper comforting.

"Within the shadow of this love,
    Loss doth transmute itself to gain;
Faith veils earth's sorrows in its light,
    And straightway lives above her pain.

"We are not losers thus; we share
    The perfect gladness of the Son,
Not conquered—for, behold, we reign;
    Conquered and Conqueror are one.

"Thy wonderful grand will, my God!
    Triumphantly I make it mine;
And faith shall breathe her glad 'Amen'
    To every dear command of Thine.

"Beneath the splendour of Thy choice,
    Thy perfect choice for me, I rest;
Outside it now I dare not live,
    Within it I must needs be blest.

"Meanwhile my spirit anchors calm
    In grander regions still than this;
The fair, far-shining latitudes
    Of that yet unexplorèd bliss.

"Then may Thy perfect, glorious will
    Be evermore fulfilled in me,
And make my life an answ'ring chord
    Of glad, responsive harmony.

"Oh! it is life indeed to live
    Within this kingdom strangely sweet;
And yet we fear to enter in,
    And linger with unwilling feet.

"We fear this wondrous rule of Thine,
    Because we have not reached Thy heart;
Not venturing our all on Thee,
    We may not know how good Thou art."

JEAN SOPHIA PIGOTT

CHAPTER X.

Our Hearts Kept for Jesus.

"Keep my heart; it is Thine own;
It is now Thy royal throne."

"IT is a good thing that the heart be established with grace," and yet some of us go on as if it were not a good thing even to hope for it to be so.

We should be ashamed to say that we had behaved treacherously to a friend; that we had played him false again and again; that we had said scores of times what we did not really mean; that we had professed and promised what, all the while, we had no sort of purpose of performing. We should be ready to go off by next ship to New Zealand rather than calmly own to all this, or rather than ever face our friends again after we had owned it. And yet we are not ashamed (some of us) to say that we are always dealing treacherously with our Lord; nay, more, we own it with an inexplicable complacency, as if there were a kind of virtue in saying how fickle and faithless and desperately wicked our hearts are; and we actually plume ourselves on the easy confession, which we think proves our humility, and which does not lower us in the eyes of others, nor in our own eyes, half so much as if we had to say, "I have told a story," or, "I have broken my promise." Nay, more, we have not the slightest hope, and therefore not the smallest intention of aiming at an utterly different state of things. Well for us if we do not go a step farther, and call those by hard and false names who do seek to have an established heart, and who believe that as the Lord meant what He said when He promised, "*No* good thing will He withhold from them that walk uprightly," so He will not withhold *this* good thing.

Prayer must be based upon promise, but, thank God, His promises are always broader than our prayers. No fear of building inverted pyramids here, for Jesus Christ is the foundation, and this and all the other " promises of God in Him are yea, and in Him Amen, unto the glory of God by us." So it shall be unto His glory to fulfil this one to us, and to answer our prayer for a "kept" or "established" heart. And its fulfilment shall work out His glory, not in spite of us, but "*by* us."

We find both the means and the result of the keeping in the 112th Psalm: "His heart is fixed." Whose heart? An angel? A saint in glory? No! Simply the heart of the man that feareth the Lord, and delighteth greatly in His commandments. Therefore yours and mine, as God would have them be; just the normal idea of a God-fearing heart, nothing extremely and hopelessly beyond attainment.

"Fixed." How does that tally with the deceitfulness and waywardness and fickleness about which we really talk as if we were rather proud of them than utterly ashamed of them?

Does our heavenly Bridegroom expect nothing more of us? Does His mighty, all-constraining love intend to do no more for us than to leave us in this deplorable state, when He is undoubtedly able to heal the desperately wicked heart (compare verses 9 and 14 of Jeremiah 17), to rule the wayward one with His peace, and to establish the fickle one with His grace? Are we not "without excuse"?

"Fixed, trusting in the Lord." Here is the means of the fixing—trust. He works the trust in us by sending the Holy Spirit to reveal God in Christ to us as absolutely, infinitely worthy of our trust. When we "see Jesus" by Spirit-wrought faith, we cannot but trust Him; we distrust our hearts more truly than ever before, but we trust our Lord entirely, because we trust Him *only*. For, entrusting our trust to Him, we know that He is able to keep that which we commit (*i.e.* entrust) to Him. It is His own way of winning and fixing our hearts for Himself. Is it not a beautiful one? Thus "his heart is established." But we have not quite faith enough to believe that. So what is the very first doubting, and therefore sad, thought that crops up? "Yes, but I am *afraid* it will not remain fixed."

That is *your* thought. Now see what is God's thought about the case. "His heart is established, he shall not be afraid."

Is not that enough? What *is*, if such plain and yet divine words are not? Well, the Gracious One bears with us, and gives line upon line to His poor little children. And so He says, "The peace of God, which passeth all understanding, shall keep your hearts and minds, through Christ Jesus." And again, "Thy thoughts shall be established." And again, "Thou wilt keep him in perfect peace, whose mind is stayed on Thee, because he trusteth it Thee."

And to prove to us that these promises can be realized in present experience, He sends down to us through nearly 3000 years the words of the man who prayed, "Create in me a clean heart, O God," and lets us hear twice over the new song put by the same Holy Spirit into his mouth: "My heart is fixed, O God, my heart is fixed" (Psalm 57:7, 108:1).

The heart that is established in Christ is also established for Christ. It becomes His royal throne, no longer occupied by His foe, no longer tottering and unstable. And then we see the beauty and preciousness of the promise, "He shall be a Priest upon His throne." Not only reigning, but atoning. Not only ruling, but cleansing. Thus the throne is established "in mercy," but by righteousness."

I think we lose ground sometimes by parleying with the tempter. We have no business to parley with an usurper. The throne is no longer his when we have surrendered it to our Lord Jesus. And why should we allow him to argue with us for one instant, as if it were still an open question? Don't listen; simply tell him that Jesus Christ *is* on the long-disputed throne, and no more about it, but turn at once to your King and claim the glorious protection of His sovereignty over you. It is a splendid reality, and you will find it so. He will not abdicate and leave you kingless and defenceless. For verily, "The Lord *is* our King; He will save us" (Isaiah 33:22).

Our hearts are naturally—		*God can make them—*	
Evil	Hebrews 3:12	Clean	Psalm 51:10
Desperately wicked	Jeremiah 17:9	Good	Luke 8:15
Weak	Ezekiel 16:30	Fixed	Psalm 112:7
Deceitful . . .	Jeremiah 17:9	Faithful . . .	Nehemiah 9:8
Deceived . . .	Isaiah 44:20	Understanding	1 Kings 3:9
Double	Psalm 12:2	Honest	Luke 8:15
Impenitent . . .	Romans 2:5	Contrite . . .	Psalm 51:17
Rebellious . . .	Jeremiah 5:23	True	Hebrews 10:22
Hard	Ezekiel 3:7	Soft	Job 23:16
Stony	Ezekiel 11:19	New	Ezekiel 18:31
Froward . . .	Proverbs 17:20	Sound	Psalms 119:80
Despiteful . . .	Ezekiel 25:15	Glad	Psalm 16:9
Stout	Isaiah 10:12	Established . .	Psalm 112:8
Haughty . . .	Proverbs 18:12	Tender . . .	Ephesians 4:32
Proud	Proverbs 21:4	Pure	Matthew 5:8
Perverse . . .	Proverbs 12:8	Perfect . . .	1 Chronicles 29:9
Foolish	Romans 1:21	Wise	Proverbs 11:29

CHAPTER XI.

Our Love Kept for Jesus.

"Keep my love; my Lord, I pour
At Thy feet its treasure-store."

NOT as a mere echo from the morning-gilded shore of Tiberias, but as an ever new, ever sounding note of divinest power, come the familiar words to each of us, "Lovest thou Me?" He says it who has loved us with an everlasting love. He says it who has died for us. He says it who has washed us from our sins in His own blood. He says it who has waited for our love, waited patiently all through our coldness.

And if by His grace we have said, "Take my love," which of us has not felt that part of His very answer has been to make us see how little there was to take, and how little of that little has been kept for Him? And yet we *do* love Him! He knows that! The very mourning and longing to love Him more proves it. But we want more than that, and so does our Lord.

He has created us to love. We have a sealed treasure of love, which either remains sealed, and then gradually dries up and wastes away, or is unsealed and poured out, and yet is the fuller and not the emptier for the outpouring. The more love we give, the more we have to give. So far it is only natural. But when the Holy Spirit reveals the love of Christ, and sheds abroad the love of God in our hearts, this natural love is penetrated with a new principle, as it discovers a new Object. Everything that it beholds in that Object gives it new depth and new colours. As it sees the holiness, the beauty, and the glory, it takes the deep hues of conscious sinfulness, unworthiness, and nothingness. As it sees even a glimpse of the love that passeth knowledge, it takes the glow of wonder and gratitude. And when it sees that love drawing close to its deepest need with blood-purchased pardon, it is intensified and stirred, and there is no more time for weighing and measuring; we must pour it out, all there is of it, with our tears, at the feet that were pierced for love of us.

And what then? Has the flow grown gradually slower and shallower? Has our Lord reason to say, "My brethren have dealt deceitfully as a brook, and as a stream of brooks they pass away"? It is humiliating to have found that we could not keep on loving Him, as we loved in that remembered hour when "Thy time was the time of love." We have proved that we were not able. Let this be only the stepping-stone to proving that He is able!

There will have been a cause, as we shall see if we seek it honestly. It was not that we really poured out all our treasure, and so it naturally came to an end. We let it be secretly diverted into other channels. We began keeping back a little part of the price for something else. We looked away from, instead of looking away unto Jesus. We did not entrust Him with our love, and ask Him to keep it for Himself.

And what has He to say to us? Ah, He upbraideth not. Listen! "Thus saith the Lord, I remember thee, the kindness of thy youth, the love of thine espousals." Can any words be more tender, more touching, to you, to me? Forgetting all the sin, all the backsliding, all the coldness, casting all that into the unreturning depths of the sea, He says He remembers that hour when we first said, "Take my love." He remembers it now, at this minute. He has written it for ever on His infinite memory, where the past is as the present.

His own love is unchangeable, so it could never be His wish or will that we should thus drift away from Him. Oh, "Come and let us return unto the Lord!" But is there any hope that, thus returning, our flickering love may be kept from again failing? Hear what He says: "And I will betroth thee unto Me for ever." And again: "Thou *shalt* abide *for Me* many days; so will I also be for thee." Shall we trust His word or not? Is it worthy of our acceptation or not? Oh, rest on this word of the King, and let Him from this day have the keeping of your love, and He will keep it!

The love of Christ is not an absorbing, but a radiating love. The more we love Him, the more we shall most certainly love others. Some have not much natural power of loving, but the love of Christ will strengthen it. Some have had the springs of love dried up by some terrible earthquake. They will find "fresh springs" in Jesus, and the gentle flow will be purer and deeper than the old torrent could ever be. Some have been satisfied that it should rush in a narrow channel, but He will cause it to overflow into many another, and widen its course of blessing. Some have spent it all on their God-given dear ones. Now He is come whose right it is; and yet in the fullest resumption of that right, He is so gracious that He puts back an even larger measure of the old love into our hand, sanctified with His own love, and energized with His blessing, and strengthened with His new commandment, "That ye love one another, as I have loved you."

In that always very interesting part, called a "Corner for Difficulties," of that always very interesting magazine, *Woman's Work*, the question has been discussed, "When does love become idolatry? Is it the experience of Christians that the coming in of a new object of affection interferes with entire consecration to God?" I should like to quote the many excellent answers in full, but must only refer my readers to the number for March 1879. One replies: "It seems to me that He who is love would not give us an object for our love unless He saw that our hearts needed expansion; and if the love is consecrated, and the friendship takes its stand in Christ, there is no need for the fear that it will become idolatry. Let the love on both sides *be given to God to keep*, and however much it may grow, the source from which it springs must yet be greater." Perhaps I may be pardoned for giving, at the same writer's suggestion, a quotation from *Under the Surface* on this subject. Eleanor says to Beatrice:—

"I tremble when I think
How much I love him; but I turn away
From thinking of it, just to love him more;—
Indeed, I fear, too much."
"Dear Eleanor,
Do you love him as much as Christ loves us?
Let your lips answer me."
"Why ask me, dear?
Our hearts are finite, Christ is infinite."
"Then, till you reach the standard of that love,
Let neither fears nor well-meant warning voice
Distress you with 'too much.' For He hath said
How much—and who shall dare to change His measure?—
'*That ye should love* AS *I have loved you.*'
O sweet command, that goes so far beyond
The mightiest impulse of the tenderest heart!
A bare permission had been much; but He
Who knows our yearnings and our fearfulness,
Chose graciously to *bid* us do the thing
That makes our earthly happiness,
A limit that we need not fear to pass,
Because we cannot. Oh, the breadth and length,
And depth and height of love that passeth knowledge!

Yet Jesus said, 'As I have loved you.'"
"O Beatrice, I long to feel the sunshine
That this should bring; but there are other words
Which fall in chill eclipse. 'Tis written, 'Keep
Yourselves from idols.' How shall I obey?"
"Oh, not by loving less, but loving more.
It is not that we love our precious ones
Too much, but God too little. As the lamp
A miner bears upon his shadowed brow
Is only dazzling in the grimy dark,
And has no glare against the summer sky,
So, set the tiny torch of our best love
In the great sunshine of the love of God,
And, though full fed and fanned, it casts no shade
And dazzles not, o'erflowed with mightier light."

There is no love so deep and wide as that which is kept for Jesus. It flows both fuller and farther when it flows only through Him. Then, too, it will be a power for Him. It will always be unconsciously working for Him. In drawing others to ourselves by it, we shall be necessarily drawing them nearer to the fountain of our love, never drawing them away from it. It is the great magnet of His love which alone can draw any heart to Him; but when our own are thoroughly yielded to its mighty influence, they will be so magnetized that He will condescend to use them in this way.

Is it not wonderful to think that the Lord Jesus will not only accept and keep, but actually use our love?

"Of Thine own have we given Thee," for "we love Him because He first loved us."

Set apart to love Him,
And His love to know;
Not to waste affection
On a passing show;
Called to give Him life and heart,
Called to pour the hidden treasure,
That none other claims to measure,
Into His belovèd hand! thrice blessèd "set apart"!

CHAPTER XII.

Our Selves Kept for Jesus.

"Keep my self, that I may be
Ever, only, all for Thee."

"FOR THEE!" That is the beginning and the end of the whole matter of consecration.

There was a prelude to its "endless song,"—a prelude whose theme is woven into every following harmony in the new anthem of consecrated life: "The Son of God, who loved me, and gave Himself *for me.*" Out of the realized "for me," grows the practical "for Thee!" If the former is a living root, the latter will be its living fruit.

"For *Thee!*" This makes the difference between forced or formal, and therefore unreasonable service, and the "reasonable service" which is the beginning of the perfect service where they see His face. This makes the difference between slave work and free work. For Thee, my Redeemer; for Thee who hast spoken to my heart; for Thee, who hast done for me—*what?* Let us each pause, and fill up that blank with the great things the Lord hath done for us. For Thee, who art to me—*what?* Fill that up too, before Him! For Thee, my Saviour Jesus, my Lord and my God!

And what is to be for Him? My self. We talk sometimes as if, whatever else could be subdued unto Him, self could never be. Did St. Paul forget to mention this important exception to the "all things" in Philippians 3:21? David said: "Bless the Lord, O my soul, *and all that is within me,* bless His Holy Name." Did he, too, unaccountably forget to mention that he only meant all that was within him, *except* self? If not, then self must be among the "all things" which the Lord Jesus Christ is able to subdue unto Himself, and which are to "bless His Holy Name." It is Self which, once His most treacherous foe, is now by full and glad surrender, His own soldier—coming over from the rebel camp into the royal army. It is not some one else, some temporarily possessing spirit, which says within us, "Lord, Thou knowest that I love Thee," but our true and very self, only changed and renewed by the power of the Holy Ghost. And when we do that we would not, we know that "it is no more I that do it, but sin that dwelleth in me." Our true self is the new self, taken and won by the love of God, and kept by the power of God.

Yes, "kept!" There is the promise on which we ground our prayer; or, rather, one of the promises. For, search and look for your own strengthening and comfort, and you will find it repeated in every part of the Bible, from "I am with thee, and will keep thee," in Genesis, to "I also will keep thee from the hour of temptation," in Revelation.

And kept *for Him!* Why should it be thought a thing incredible with you, when it is only the fulfilling of His own eternal purpose in creating us? "This people have I formed *for Myself*." Not ultimately only, but presently and continually; for He says, "Thou shalt abide *for Me*"; and, "He that remaineth, even he shall be *for our God*." Are you one of His people by faith in Jesus Christ? Then see what you are to Him. You, personally and individually, are part of the Lord's portion (Deuteronomy 32:9) and of His inheritance (1 Kings 8:53, and Ephesians 1:18). His portion and inheritance would not be complete without you; you are His peculiar treasure (Exodus 19:5); "a *special* people" (how warm, and loving, and natural that expression is!) "*unto Himself*" (Deuteronomy 7:6). Would you call it "keeping," if you had a "special" treasure, a darling little child, for instance, and let it run wild into all sorts of dangers all day long, sometimes at your side, and sometimes out in the street, with only the intention of fetching it safe home at night? If ye then, being evil, would know better, and do better, than that, how much more shall our Lord's keeping be true, and tender, and continual, and effectual when He declares us to be His peculiar treasure, purchased (see 1 Peter 2:9, margin) for Himself at such unknown cost!

> He will keep what thus He sought,
> Safely guard the dearly bought;
> Cherish that which He did choose,
> Always love and never lose.

I know what some of us are thinking. "Yes, I see it all plainly enough in theory, but in practise I find I am not kept. Self goes over to the other camp again and again. It is not all for Jesus, though I have asked and wished for it to be so." Dear friends, the "all" must be sealed with "only." Are you willing to be "*only*" for Jesus? You have not given "all" to Jesus while you are not quite ready to be "*only*" for Him. And it is no use to talk about "ever" while we have not settled the "only" and the "all." You cannot be "for Him," in the full and blessed sense while you are partly "for" anything or any one else. For "the Lord hath *set apart* him that is godly for Himself." You see, the "for Himself" hinges upon the "set apart." There is no consecration without separation. If you are mourning over want of realized consecration, will you look humbly and sincerely into *this* point? "A garden *enclosed* is my sister, my spouse," saith the Heavenly Bridegroom.

Set apart for Jesus!
Is not this enough,
Though the desert prospect
Open wild and rough?
Set apart for His delight,
Chosen for His holy pleasure,
Sealed to be His special treasure!
Could we choose a nobler joy?—and would we,
if we might?[1]

But yielding, by His grace, to this blessed setting apart for Himself, "The Lord shall *establish* thee an holy people unto Himself, as He hath sworn unto thee." Can there be a stronger promise? Just obey and trust His word now, and yield yourselves now unto God, "that He may establish thee *to-day* for a people unto Himself." Commit the keeping of your souls to Him in well-doing, as unto a faithful Creator, being persuaded that He is ABLE TO KEEP that which you commit to Him.

Now, Lord, I give myself to Thee,
I would be wholly Thine,
As Thou hast given Thyself to me,
And Thou art wholly mine;
O take me, seal me for Thine own,
Thine altogether, Thine alone.

Here comes in once more that immeasurably important subject of our influence. For it is not what we say or do, so much as what we *are*, that influences others. We have heard this, and very likely repeated it again and again, but have we seen it to be inevitably linked with the great question of this chapter? I do not know anything which, thoughtfully considered, makes us realize

---

[1] *Loyal Responses*, the Second Day, page 352 of Volume II of the Havergal edition.

more vividly the need and the importance of our whole selves being kept for Jesus. Any part not wholly committed, and not wholly kept, must hinder and neutralize the real influence for Him of all the rest. If we ourselves are kept all for Jesus, then our influence will be all kept for Him too. If not, then, however much we may wish and talk and try, we cannot throw our full weight into the right scale. And just in so far as it is not in the one scale, it must be in the other; weighing against the little which we have tried to put in the right one, and making the short weight still shorter.

So large a proportion of it is entirely involuntary, while yet the responsibility of it is so enormous, that our helplessness comes out in exceptionally strong relief, while our past debt in this matter is simply incalculable. Are we feeling this a little? getting just a glimpse, down the misty defiles of memory, of the neutral influence, the wasted influence, the mistaken influence, the actually wrong influence which has marked the ineffaceable although untraceable course? And all the while we owed Him all that influence! It *ought* to have been all for Him! We have nothing to say. But what has our Lord to say? "I forgave thee all *that* debt!"

Then, after that forgiveness which must come first, there comes a thought of great comfort in our freshly felt helplessness, rising out of the very thing that makes us realize this helplessness. Just *because* our influence is to such a great extent involuntary and unconscious, we may rest assured that if we ourselves are truly kept for Jesus, this will be, as a quite natural result, kept for Him also. It cannot be otherwise, for as is the fountain, so will be the flow; as the spring, so the action; as the impulse, so the communicated motion, Thus there may be, and in simple trust there will be, a quiet rest about it, a relief from all sense of strain and effort, a fulfilling of the words, "For he that is entered into his rest, he also hath ceased from his own works, as God did from His." It will not be a matter of *trying* to have good influence, but just of *having* its as naturally and constantly as the magnetized bar.

Another encouraging thought should follow. Of ourselves we may have but little weight, no particular talents or position or anything else to put into the scale; but let us remember that again and again God has shown that the influence of a very average life, when once really consecrated to Him, may outweigh that of almost any number of merely professing Christians. Such lives are like Gideon's three hundred, carrying not even the ordinary weapons of war, but only trumpets and lamps and empty pitchers, by whom the Lord wrought great deliverance, while He did not use the others at all. For He hath chosen the weak things of the world to confound the things which are mighty.

Should not all this be additional motive for desiring that our *whole* selves should be taken and kept?

I know that whatsoever God doeth, it shall be for ever. Therefore we may rejoicingly say "ever" as well as "only" and "all for Thee!" For the Lord is our Keeper, and He is the Almighty and the Everlasting God, with whom is no variableness, neither shadow of turning. He will never change His mind about keeping us, and no man is able to pluck us out of His hand. Neither will Christ let us pluck ourselves out of His hand, for He says, "Thou *shalt* abide for Me many days." And He that keepeth us will not slumber. Once having undertaken His vineyard, He will keep it night and day, till all the days and nights are over, and we know the full meaning of the salvation ready to be revealed in the last time, unto which we are kept by His power.

And then, for ever for Him! passing from the gracious keeping by faith for this little while, to the glorious keeping in His presence for all eternity! For ever fulfilling the object for which He formed us and chose us, we showing forth His praise, and He showing the exceeding riches of His grace in His kindness towards us in the ages to come! *He for us, and we for Him for ever!* Oh, how little we can grasp this! Yet this is the fruition of being "kept for Jesus!"

> Set apart for ever
> For Himself alone!
> Now we see our calling
> Gloriously shown.
> Owning, with no secret dread,
> This our holy separations
> Now the crown of consecration[1]
> Of the Lord our God shall rest upon our willing head.

[1] Numbers 6:7.

CHAPTER XIII.

Christic for Us.

"So will I also be for Thee."—Hosea 3:3.

THE typical promise, "Thou shalt abide for Me many days," is indeed a marvel of love. For it is given to the most undeserving, described under the strongest possible figure of utter worthlessness and treacherousness,—the woman beloved, yet an adulteress.

The depth of the abyss shows the length of the line that has fathomed it, yet only the length of the line reveals the real depth of the abyss. The sin shows the love, and the love reveals the sin. The Bible has few words more touching, though seldom quoted, than those just preceding this wonderful promise: "The love of the Lord toward the children of Israel, who look to other gods, and love flagons of wine." Put that into the personal application which no doubt underlies it, and say, "The love of the Lord toward me, who have looked away from Him, with wandering, faithless eyes, to other helps and hopes, and have loved earthly joys and sought earthly gratifications,—the love of the Lord toward even me!" And then hear Him saying in the next verse, "So I bought her to Me"; stooping to do *that* in His unspeakable condescension of love, not with the typical silver and barley, but with the precious blood of Christ. Then, having thus loved us, and rescued us, and bought us with a price indeed, He says, still under the same figure, "Thou shalt abide for Me many days."

This is both a command and a pledge. But the very pledge implies our past unfaithfulness, and the proved need of even our own part being undertaken by the ever patient Lord. He Himself has to guarantee our faithfulness, because there is no other hope of our continuing faithful. Well may such love win our full and glad surrender, and such a promise win our happy and confident trust!

But He says more. He says, "So will I also be for thee!" And this seems an even greater marvel of love, as we observe how He meets every detail of our consecration with this wonderful word.[1]

1. *His Life* "for thee!" "The Good Shepherd giveth His life for the sheep." Oh, wonderful gift! not promised, but *given*; not to friends, but to enemies. Given without condition, without reserve, without return. Himself unknown and unloved, His gift unsought and unasked, He gave His life for thee; a more than royal bounty—the greatest gift that Deity could devise. Oh, grandeur of love! "I lay down My life for the sheep!" And we for whom He gave it have held back, and hesitated to give our lives, not even *for* Him (He has not asked us to do that), but *to* Him! But that is past, and He has tenderly pardoned the unloving, ungrateful reserve, and has graciously accepted the poor little fleeting breath and speck of dust which was all we had to offer. And now His precious death and His glorious life are all "for thee."

2. *His Eternity* "for thee." All we can ask Him to take are days and moments—the little span given us as it is given, and of this only the present in deed and the future in will. As for the past, in so far as we did not give it to Him, it is too late; we can never give it now! But His past was given to us, though ours was not given to Him. Oh, what a tremendous debt does this show us!

Away back in the dim depths of past eternity, "or ever the earth and the world were made," His divine existence in the bosom of His Father was all "for thee," purposing and planning "for thee," receiving and holding the promise of eternal life "for thee."

Then the thirty-three years among sinners on this sinful earth: do we think enough of the slowly-wearing days and nights, the heavyfooted hours, the never-hastening minutes, that went to make up those thirty-three years of trial and humiliation? We all know how slowly time passes when suffering and sorrow are near, and there is no reason to suppose that our Master was exempted from this part of our infirmities.

Then His present is "for thee." Even now He "liveth to make intercession"; even now He "thinketh upon me"; even now He "knoweth," He "careth," He "loveth."

Then, only to think that His whole eternity will be "for thee!" Millions of ages of unfoldings of all His love, and of ever new declarings of His Father's name to His brethren. Think of it! and can we ever hesitate to give *all* our poor little hours to His service?

[1] The remainder of this chapter is printed in a little penny book, entitled, *I also for Thee*, by F. R. H., published by Caswell, Birmingham, and by Nisbet & Co. [See pages 677–685 of Volume II of the Havergal edition.]

3. *His Hands* "for thee." Literal hands; literally pierced, when the whole weight of His quivering frame hung from their torn muscles and bared nerves; literally uplifted in parting blessing. Consecrated, priestly hands; "filled" hands (Exodus 28:41, 29:9, etc., margin)—filled once with His great offering, and now with gifts and blessings "for thee." Tender hands, touching and healing, lifting and leading with gentlest care. Strong hands, upholding and defending. Open hands, filling with good and satisfying desire (Psalm 104:28, and 145:16). Faithful hands, restraining and sustaining. "His left hand is under my head, and His right hand doth embrace me."

4. *His Feet* "for thee." They were weary very often, they were wounded and bleeding once. They made clear footprints as He went about doing good, and as He went up to Jerusalem to suffer; and these "blessed steps of His most holy life," both as substitution and example, were "for thee." Our place of waiting and learning, of resting and loving, is at His feet. And still those "blessed feet" are and shall be "for thee," until He comes again to receive us unto Himself, until and when the word is fulfilled, "They shall walk with me in white."

5. *His Voice* "for thee." The "Voice of my beloved that knocketh, saying, Open to me, my sister, my love"; the Voice that His sheep "hear" and "know," and that calls out the fervent response, "Master, say on!" This is not all. It was the literal voice of the Lord Jesus which uttered that one echoless cry of desolation on the Cross "for thee," and it will be His own literal voice which will say, "Come, ye blessed!" to thee. And that same tender and "glorious Voice" has literally sung and will sing "for thee." I think He consecrated song for us, and made it a sweet and sacred thing for ever, when He Himself "sang an hymn," the very last thing before He went forth to consecrate suffering for us. That was not His last song. "The Lord thy God ... will joy over thee with singing." And the time is coming when He will not only sing "for thee" or "over thee," but with thee. He says He will! "In the midst of the church will I sing praise unto Thee." Now what a magnificent glimpse of joy this is! "Jesus Himself leading the praises of His brethren,"[1] and we ourselves singing not merely in such a chorus, but with such a leader! If "singing for Jesus" is such delight here, what will this "singing *with* Jesus" be? Surely song may well be a holy thing to us henceforth.

---

[1] See A. Newton on the Epistle to the Hebrews, ch. 2. ver. 12.

6. *His Lips* "for thee." Perhaps there is no part of our consecration which it is so difficult practically to realize, and in which it is, therefore, so needful to recollect—"I also for thee." It is often helpful to read straight through one or more of the Gospels with a special thought on our mind, and see how much bears upon it. When we read one through with this thought,—"His *lips* for me!"—wondering, verse by verse, at the grace which was poured into them, and the gracious words which fell from them, wondering more and more at the cumulative force and infinite wealth of tenderness and power and wisdom and love flowing from them, we cannot but desire that our lips and all the fruit of them should be wholly for Him. "For thee" they were opened in blessing; "for thee" they were closed when He was led as a lamb to the slaughter. And whether teaching, warning, counsel, comfort, or encouragement, commandments in whose keeping there is a great reward, or promises which exceed all we ask or think—all the precious fruit of His lips is "for thee" really and truly *meant* "for thee."

7. *His Wealth* "for thee." "Though He was rich, yet for our sakes He became poor, that ye through His poverty might be made rich." Yes, "through His poverty" the unsearchable riches of Christ are "for thee." Sevenfold riches are mentioned; and these are no untainted treasure or sealed reserve, but all ready coined for our use, and stamped with His own image and superscription, and poured freely into the hand of faith. The mere list is wonderful. "Riches of goodness," "riches of forbearance and long-suffering," "riches both of wisdom and knowledge," "riches of mercy," "exceeding riches of grace," and "riches of glory." And His own Word says, "All are yours!" Glance on in faith, and think of eternity flowing on and on beyond the mightiest sweep of imagination, and realize that all "His riches in glory" and "the riches of His glory" are and shall be "for thee!" In view of this, shall we care to reserve anything that rust doth corrupt for ourselves?

8. *His "treasures of wisdom and knowledge"* "for thee." First, used for our behalf and benefit. Why did He expend such immeasurable might of mind upon a world which is to be burnt up, but that He would fit it perfectly to be, not the home, but the school of His children? The infinity of His skill is such that the most powerful intellects find a lifetime too short to penetrate a little way into a few secrets of some one small department of His working. If we turn to Providence, it is quite enough to take only one's own life, and look at it microscopically and telescopically, and marvel at the treasures of wisdom lavished upon its details, ordering and shaping and fitting the tiny confused bits into the true mosaic which He means it to be. Many a little thing in our lives reveals the same

Mind which, according to a well-known and very beautiful illustration, adjusted a perfect proportion in the delicate hinges of the snowdrop and the droop of its bell, with the mass of the globe and the force of gravitation. How kind we think it if a very talented friend spends a little of his thought and power of mind in teaching us or planning for us! Have we been grateful for the infinite thought and wisdom which our Lord has expended upon us and our creation, preservation, and redemption?

Secondly, to be shared with us. He says, "All that I have is thine." He holds nothing back, reserves nothing from His dear children, and what we cannot receive now He is keeping for us. He gives us "hidden riches of secret places" now, but by and by He will give us more, and the glorified intellect will be filled continually out of His treasures of wisdom and knowledge. But the sanctified intellect will be, must be, used for Him, and only for Him, now!

9. *His Will* "for thee." Think first of the *infinite might* of that will; the first great law and the first great force of the universe, from which alone every other law and every other force has sprung, and to which all are subordinate. "He worketh all things after the counsel of His own will." "He doeth according to His will in the army of heaven, and among the inhabitants of the earth." Then think of the *infinite mysteries* of that will. For ages and generations the hosts of heaven have wonderingly watched its vouchsafed unveilings and its sublime developments, and still they are waiting, watching, and wondering.

Creation and Providence are but the whisper of its power, but Redemption is its music, and praise is the echo which shall yet fill His temple. The whisper and the music, yes, and "the thunder of His power," are all "for thee." For what is "the good pleasure of His will"? (Ephesians 1:5). Oh, what a grand list of blessings purposed, provided, purchased, and possessed, all flowing to us out of it! And nothing but blessings, nothing but privileges, which we never should have imagined, and which, even when revealed, we are "slow of heart to believe"; nothing but what should even now fill us "with joy unspeakable and full of glory!"

Think of this will as always and altogether on our side—always working for us, and in us, and with us, if we will only let it; think of it as always and only synonymous with infinitely wise and almighty love; think of it as undertaking all for us, from the great work of our eternal salvation down to the momentary details of guidance and supply, and do we not feel utter shame and self-abhorrence at *ever* having hesitated for an instant to give up our tiny, feeble, blind will, to be—not crushed, not even bent, but *blent* with His glorious and perfect Will?

10. *His Heart* "for thee." "Behold... He is mighty... in heart," said Job (Job 36:5, margin). And this mighty and tender heart is "for thee!" If He had only stretched forth His hand to save us from bare destruction, and said, "My hand for thee!" how could we have praised Him enough? But what shall we say of the unspeakably marvellous condescension which says, "Thou hast ravished (margin, *taken away*) my heart, my sister, my spouse!" The very fountain of His divine life, and light, and love, the very centre of His being, is given to His beloved ones, who are not only "set as a seal upon His heart," but taken into His heart, so that our life is hid there, and we dwell there in the very centre of all safety, and power, and love, and glory. What will be the revelation of "that day," when the Lord Jesus promises, "Ye shall know that I am in my Father, *and ye in Me*"? For He implies that we do not yet know it, and that our present knowledge of this dwelling in Him is not knowledge at all compared with what He is going to show us about it.

Now shall we, can we, reserve any corner of our hearts from Him?

11. *His Love* "for thee." Not a passive, possible love, but outflowing, yes, *outpouring* of the real, glowing, personal love of His mighty and tender heart. Love not as an attribute, a quality, a latent force, but an acting, moving, reaching, touching, and grasping power. Love, not a cold, beautiful, far-off star, but a sunshine that comes and enfolds us, making us warm and glad, and strong and bright and fruitful.

His love! What manner of love is it? What should be quoted to prove or describe it? First the whole Bible with its mysteries and marvels of redemption, then the whole book of Providence and the whole volume of creation. Then add to these the unknown records of eternity past and the unknown glories of eternity to come, and then let the immeasurable quotation be sung by "angels and archangels, and all the company of heaven," with all the harps of God, and still that love will be untold, still it will be "the love of Christ that passeth knowledge."

But it is "for thee!"

12. *Himself* "for thee." "Christ also hath loved us, and given Himself for us." "The Son of God... loved me, and gave Himself for me." Yes, Himself! What is the Bride's true and central treasure? What calls forth the deepest, brightest, sweetest thrill of love and praise? Not the Bridegroom's priceless gifts, not the robe of His resplendent righteousness, not the dowry of unsearchable riches, not the magnificence of the palace home to which He is bringing her, not the glory which she shall share with Him, but HIMSELF! Jesus Christ, "who His

own self bare our sins in His own body on the tree"; "this same Jesus" "whom having not seen, ye love"; the Son of God, and the Man of Sorrows; my Saviour, my Friend, my Master, my King, my Priest, my Lord and my God—He says, "*I* also for thee!" What an "*I*"! What power and sweetness we feel in it, so different from any human "*I*," for all His Godhead and all His manhood are concentrated in it, and all "for thee!"

And not only "all," but "*ever*" for thee. His unchangeableness is the seal upon every attribute; He will be "this same Jesus" for ever. How can mortal mind estimate this enormous promise? How can mortal heart conceive what is enfolded in these words, "I also for thee"?

One glimpse of its fulness and glory, and we feel that henceforth it must be, shall be, and by His grace *will* be our true-hearted, whole-hearted cry—

> Take *myself*, and I will be
> *Ever*, ONLY, ALL for Thee!

STARLIGHT THROUGH THE SHADOWS,

And Other Gleams from the King's Word.

BY THE LATE

FRANCES RIDLEY HAVERGAL.

"Until the day break, and the shadows flee away."—Song 2:17.

Fifty-eighth Thousand.

London:

JAMES NISBET & CO.

21 BERNERS STREET.

PREFACE.

"Work for 1879, if the Lord will. To write 'Starlight through the Shadows,' a daily book for Invalids." Such was the intention of my dear sister, F. R. H. Having herself passed through the shadows of sickness and sorrow, she sought to bring some "starry promise sure," which might be more welcome, to the feeble eye, than the dazzling rays of brighter promises.

In answer to a suggestion, that she should write on some other subjects, her characteristic reply was: "I don't think I have got any real commission to write anything at all for next autumn, except the invalid book. I believe I am going off the line of my especial calling if once I begin to think of writing as a matter of business and success and cheque, and all that; and I can't expect the same blessing in it. And so, though of course it stands to reason that the invalid book must have a very limited circulation compared to the others, I shall be much happier doing that; and I believe I shall have more real, *i.e.* spiritual results from it, than if I set myself to do any others, because I do think God gave me the thought to do this one. I have felt so very strongly and sweetly hitherto, that my pen was to be used *only* for the Master, that I am very fearful of getting the least out of the course in which I have felt His blessing." (*March* 1879.)

Only eleven chapters were written, when for her all shadows fled away, and were exchanged for the shadowless splendour of the very Light of Light!

To complete a seventh and last volume of F. R. H.'s Royal series, selections have been made from her unpublished manuscripts.

My beloved sister's life-long interest in all missionary work seems to culminate in her "Marching Orders." By request of Mr. Eugene Stock, she wrote these papers for the *Church Missionary Gleaner* of 1879.

Outlines of addresses given at various times, with other papers, show her diligent searchings in the Scripture of truth.

May the Holy Spirit's blessing cause them to be helpful Gleams from the King's Word.

Maria V. G. Havergal.

December 14th, 1881.

CONTENTS.

CHAPTER I.

Softly and Safely.

"I will lead on softly, according as the cattle that goeth before me and the children be able to endure."—GENESIS 33:14.

THE story of Jacob's thoughtfulness for the cattle and the children is a beautiful little picture. He would not let them be overdriven even for one day. Verse 13: "My lord knoweth that the children are tender, and the flocks and herds with young are with me: and if men should overdrive them one day, all the flock will die."

He would not lead on according to what a strong man like Esau could do and expected them to do, but only according to what they were able to endure. Verse 12: "Let us take our journey, and let us go, and I will go before thee." He had had so much to do with them that he knew exactly how far they could go in a day; and he made that his only consideration in arranging the marches.

Perhaps his own halting thigh made him the more considerate for "the foot of the cattle" and "the foot of the children" (see margin). Besides, he had gone the same wilderness journey years before (chap. 29:1: "Then Jacob went on his journey, and came into the land of the people of the east"), when they were not yet in existence, and knew all about its roughness and heat and length by personal experience. And so he said, "I will lead on softly."

"For ye have not passed this way heretofore" (Joshua 3:4). We have not passed this way heretofore, but the Lord Jesus has. "For we have not an high priest which cannot be touched with the feeling of our infirmities" (Hebrews 4:15). It is all untrodden and unknown ground to us, but He knows it all by personal experience; the steep bits that take away our breath, the stony bits that make our feet ache so, the hot shadeless stretches that make us feel so exhausted, the rushing rivers that we have to pass through, Jesus has gone through it all before us. "For Himself took our infirmities and bare our sicknesses" (Matthew 8:17). "For in that He Himself hath suffered being tempted" (Hebrews 2:18).

He was wearied with His journey; "Jesus therefore, being wearied with His journey" (John 4:6). Not some but all the many waters went over Him, and yet did not quench His love. "All Thy waves and Thy billows are gone over me" (Psalm 42:7). "Many waters cannot quench love, neither can the floods drown it" (Song of Solomon 8:7).

He was made a perfect Leader by the things which He suffered. Hebrews 2:10: "To make the Captain of their salvation perfect through sufferings." Hebrews 5:8, 9: "Though He were a Son, yet learned He obedience by the things which He suffered; and being made perfect, He became the Author of eternal salvation unto all them that obey Him." For now He knows all about it, and leads us softly according as we are able to endure.

"For He knoweth our frame" (Psalm 103:14). And He does not only know, with that sort of up-on-the-shelf knowledge which is often guilty of want of thought among ourselves, but He *remembereth* that we are dust. Psalm 78:39: "For He remembered that they were but flesh." Think of that when you are tempted to question the gentleness of the leading. He is remembering all the time; and not one step will He make you take beyond what your foot is able to endure. Never mind if you think it will not be able for the step that seems to come next; either He will so strengthen it that it shall be able, or He will call a sudden halt, and you shall not have to take it at all.

Is it not restful to know that you are not answerable to any Esaus, for how much you get through, or how far you are led on in the day! "They" don't know, or, knowing, don't remember, the weakness or the drawbacks. Maybe they wonder you do not get on farther and faster, doing the work better, bearing up against the suffering or the sorrow more bravely. And maybe you feel wounded and wearied without a word being said, simply because you know they *don't* know! Then turn to the Good Shepherd in whose "feeble flock" you are, and remember that He remembers. Talk to Him about it; and if too weary even for that, then just lean on Him with whom you have to do. For "all things are naked and opened unto the eyes of Him with whom we have to do" (Hebrews 4:13). It is only when we are coming up from the wilderness, leaning on our Beloved, that we can realize how softly He is leading us. "Who is this that cometh up from the wilderness, leaning upon her Beloved?" (Song of Solomon 8:5). For if we are pulling this way and that way, straggling and struggling, and wasting our steps by little turnings aside, He may have to resort to other means to keep us in the way at all. But if we are willing to lean, we shall soon find that He is leading not only rightly, (that we never doubted,) but softly too. And leading softly will not be leading slowly. "And He led them forth by the right way" (Psalm 107:7).

Minds are differently constituted, and some do not readily grasp as a real promise what is indicated in a figure. But if the figure is a true illustration, we are sure to find the same promise somewhere else in a direct form. So if you hesitate to appropriate the promise that Jesus as your Good Shepherd "will lead on softly,' take the same thing from that familiar verse in Isaiah 40; "shall gently lead" is the very same word in the original; and in the dear old 23rd Psalm "He leadeth me" is still the same word, and might be read, "He gently, or softly, leadeth me." These are the true sayings of your God.

One sees at a glance, by referring to a Concordance, the touching fact that our Leader Himself experienced very different leading. Never once was He gently led. He was led into the wilderness to be tempted of the devil (Matthew 4:1); He was led by men filled with wrath to the brow of the hill, that they might cast Him down headlong (Luke 4:29); He was led away to Annas, led away to Caiaphas (John 18:13, Matthew 26:57); led into the council of the elders and chief priests and scribes (Luke 22:66); led to Pontius Pilate (Matthew 27:2), and into the hall of judgment (John 18:28). And then He, our Lord Jesus Christ, was led as a sheep to the slaughter (Acts 8:32); led away to be crucified! (John 19:16.) Verily, "His way was much rougher and darker than mine."

That is how Jesus was led. But as for His people, "He guided them in the wilderness like a flock, and He led them on safely, so that they feared not." (Psalm 78:52, 53).

Not only safely as to the end of the journey, but as to each step. For He employs another figure to prove this, saying that He led them "as a horse in the wilderness, that they should not stumble."[1] "As a beast goeth down into the valley, the Spirit of the Lord caused him to rest." Can you not see the steep stony path of the rocky descent into a desert valley, and the careful owner's hand leading the hesitating horse, keeping fast hold of his head, and encouraging him with tones which he can understand, till the halting place at the bottom is safely reached! "So didst Thou lead Thy people" says Isaiah. So He leadeth me! responds your heart, does it not? Softly and safely, step by step, and mile by mile, till the desert journey is over and the Father's home reached!

Then trust Him for to-day
As thine unfailing Friend,

[1] This exposition of the passage is familiar and obvious enough; but I was much interested by a friend's calling my attention to the French translation, which brings it out beautifully: "L'Esprit de l'Eternel les a conduits tout doucement, comme on conduit une bête qui descend dans une plaine. C'est ainsi que Tu as conduit Ton peuple."

And let Him lead thee all the way
 Who loveth to the end.
And let the morrow rest
 In His belovèd hand,
His good is better than our best,
 As we shall understand;
If, trusting Him who faileth never,
We rest on Him to-day, for ever!

CHAPTER II.

What Seemeth Him Good.

"Let Him do what seemeth Him good."—1 SAMUEL 3:18.

ELI spoke these words under the terrible certainty of heavy judgments upon his house, because the Lord had spoken it. But how often God's dear children tremble to say an unreserved "*Let* Him do what seemeth Him good," though they are under no such shadow of certainly coming events! It is almost easier to say it when a crushing blow has actually fallen, than when there is suspense and uncertainty as to what the Lord may be going to do. There is always more or less of this element of suspense and uncertainty. One can hardly imagine a life in which there are no clouds, little or great, within the horizon, even when the sky is clearest over head. We hold not a treasure on earth which we are sure of keeping; and we never know whether gain or loss, failure or success, ease or pain, lies before us. And if we were allowed to put our finger on the balance of uncertainties and turn it as we chose, we should be sure to defeat some ultimate aim by securing a nearer one, and prevent some greater good by grasping a lesser. I think if we were permitted to try such an experiment, we should soon grow utterly puzzled and weary, and find ourselves landed in complications of mistakes; and if we had any sense left, we should want to put it all back into our Father's hands, and say "Let Him do what seemeth *Him* good," then we should feel relieved and at rest.

Then why not be relieved and at rest at once? For "it is *the Lord*," who is going to do we know not what. That is a volume in itself,—the Lord who loves you, the Lord who thinks about you and cares for you, the Lord who understands you, the Lord who never makes a mistake, the Lord who spared not His own Son but gave Him up for you! Will you not let *Him* do what seemeth Him good? Then think *what* it is you are to let Him do. Something out of your sight, perhaps, but not out of His sight. For the original word in every case is "what is good *in His eyes.*" Those Eyes see through and through, and all round and beyond everything. So what is good in His Eyes must be absolutely and entirely good, a vast deal better than our best! There is great rest in knowing that He will do what is *right,* but He crowns the rightness with the goodness; and when we see this, the rest is crowned with gladness. Ought it, then, to be so very hard to say, "Let Him do what seemeth Him *good*"?

It is very interesting to trace out that in each recorded instance of this expression of submissive trust at a juncture of dark uncertainty the result was always something most evidently "good," in the eyes of those who ventured to say it.

First, there were the Gibeonites. They came to Joshua (who by his very name, as well as office, was a direct type of Christ), "sore afraid for their lives." But, because he had made peace with them, they said, "Behold, we are in thine hand: as it seemeth good and right unto thee to do unto us, do." A beautiful illustration of confidence based upon covenant. Now see how their trust was justified. "*So* did he unto them," that is, as it was good and right in his eyes; and the first thing was, that he "delivered them out of the hand of the children of Israel that they slew them not." And the next thing was his ascending from Gilgal to fight their battles for them, conquering five kings for them, and calling upon the sun to stand still over their city "about a whole day," so that "there was no day like that before it, or after it."

Next we find the children of Israel sold for their evil deeds, into the hands of the Philistines and Ammonites, and vexed and oppressed for eighteen years. ("Vexed and oppressed,"—does that describe your case?) They come to the Lord with bare, excuseless confession, "We have sinned," and then they cast themselves on bare undeserved mercy: "Do Thou unto us whatsoever seemeth good unto Thee." And what then? "His soul was grieved for the misery of Israel." Could anything be more humanly tender, as well as Divinely magnanimous! Is it not a lesson to come straight to His heart with any misery of which the sting is that we have brought it on ourselves, and deserved it a thousandfold? First confess the sin, and then leave the sorrows wholly in His hands, and we find Him verily "the same Lord, whose property is always to have mercy." And mercy includes help, for the Lord did not stop short at grieving over their misery; He sent Jephthah to deliver them, so that they "dwelled safe" for about thirty years. (Compare Judges 11:33 and 1 Samuel 12:11.)

Now turn to 1 Chronicles 19:13, "and let the Lord do that which is good in His sight." Here Joab finds a double army "set against him before and behind." He makes the wisest arrangements he can think of, and encourages his brother; and then he says, "and let the Lord do that which is good in His sight." And what the Lord did was to give him a splendid victory. It does not seem that he had to fight or suffer any loss at all; the Syrians and Ammonites simply fled before him: verses 15, 16. "And when the children of Ammon saw that the Syrians were fled, they likewise fled before Abishai his brother, and entered into the city. Then Joab came to Jerusalem. And when the Syrians saw that they were put to the worse before Israel, they sent messengers and drew forth the Syrians that were beyond the river."

The most touching instance however is David. "And the king said unto Zadok, carry back the ark of God into the city: if I shall find favour in the eyes of the Lord, He will bring me again and show me both it and His habitation. But if He thus say, I have no delight in thee; behold here am I, let Him do to me as seemeth good unto Him." Driven from his royal home by his own son, passing amid tears over the brook Kidron, going toward the way of the wilderness, "weary and weak handed," the wisest head in the land giving counsel against him, and the hearts of the men of Israel going after the traitor, and now losing the visible token of the presence of God Himself! I do not see how any of us could be brought to such a pass as all this! And yet he said, "Let Him do to me as seemeth good unto Him." But only a little while, and the Lord, whom He trusted so implicitly in such depths, restored to him all that seemed so nearly lost, and raised him again to royal heights of prosperity and praise.

Did not these things happen unto them for ensamples? If they, in the dim old days of type and veil, could so trust the God of Israel, should we, who have the light of the knowledge of the glory of God in the face of Jesus Christ, hesitate to utter the same expression of submissive confidence? And if He has caused such records of His gracious responses to their submission to be written, should we not take them as intended to encourage our hearts in the gloomy and dark day? See now if you cannot find something like your own case in one or other of them, and remember you have the same Saviour and the same Lord to do with. And then, venture the word! Just *let* Him do what seemeth Him good, and tell Him so! It may be you have been actually hindering deliverance and thwarting help, by not "letting" Him. Do not say, "But what difference can that make? He will do what He pleases, of course, whether I am willing or not." Not exactly that. Does it make no difference if the patient quietly lets the surgeon do what he thinks best? A remedy applied by force, or submitted to unwillingly, may be quite counteracted by fidget, or by feverishness induced or increased through setting one's self against what is prescribed or advised. The Lord's remedies do not have fair play, when we set ourselves against them. Even Omnipotence waits for the faith that will *let* it act.

"And the vessel that he made of clay was marred in the hand of the potter. So he made it again another vessel, as seemed good to the potter to make it." See Jeremiah 18:4.

If the "vessel made of clay," that was marred in the hand of the potter, could have resisted that skilful hand, how would he have been able to make it again another vessel, as it seemed good to him to make it? The unresisting clay could not help *letting* the potter remould it, into a better and permanent form; but we *can* hinder, simply by not "letting." But will you do this? For "now, O Lord, Thou art our Father, we are the clay, and Thou our Potter." Whatever may be our Potter's mysterious mouldings, or our Father's mysterious dealings (I do not mean abstract, or possible, or future; but real, and present, and pressing), let us give the one sweet answer which meets *everything*: "even so, Father, for so it seemed good in Thy sight."

> Not yet thou knowest what I do
>   Within thine own weak breast;
> To mould thee to My image true,
>   And fit thee for My rest.
> But yield thee to My loving skill;
>   The veilèd work of grace,
> From day to day progressing still,
>   It is not thine to trace.
>
> Yes, walk by faith and not by sight,
>   Fast clinging to My hand;
> Content to feel My love and might,
>   Not yet to understand.
> A little while thy course pursue,
>   Till grace to glory grow;
> *Then* what I am, and *what I do,*
>   Hereafter thou shalt know.

(*Ministry of Song.*)

CHAPTER III.

The Silence of Love.

"Rest in (*margin* 'Be silent to') the Lord."—PSALM 37:7.

A N invalid was left alone one evening for a little while. After many days of
acute pain there was a lull. "Now," she thought, "I shall be able to pray
a little." But she was too wearied out and exhausted for this; feeling that utter
weakness of mind and body which cannot be realized without actual experience,
when the very lips shrink from the exertion of a whisper, and it seems too much
effort of thought to shape even unspoken words. Only one whisper came:
"Lord Jesus, I am so tired!" She prayed no more; she could not frame even a
petition that, as she could not speak to Him, He would speak to her. But the
Lord Jesus knew all the rest; He knew how she had waited for and wanted the
sweet conscious communing with Him, the literal talking to Him and telling
Him all that was in her heart. And He knew that, although a quiet and comparatively painless hour had come, she was "so tired" that she could not think.
Very tenderly did He, who knows how to speak a word in season to the weary, choose a message in reply to that little whisper. "Be silent to the Lord!" It
came like a mother's "hush" to one whom his mother comforteth. It was quite
enough, as every Spirit-given word is; and the acquiescent silence was filled with
perfect peace. Only real friends understand silence. With a passing guest or ceremonial acquaintance you feel under an obligation to talk; you make effort to
entertain them as a matter of courtesy; you may be tired or weak, but no matter, you feel you must exert yourself. But with a very dear and intimate friend
sitting by you, there is no feeling of the kind. To be sure, you may talk if you
feel able: pouring out all sort of confidences, relieved and refreshed by the inter-
change of thoughts and sympathies. But if you are very tired, you know you do
not need to say a word. You are perfectly understood, and you know it. You can
enjoy the mere fact of your friend's presence, and find that does you more good

than conversation. The sense of that present and sympathetic affection rests you more than any words. And your friend takes it as the highest proof of your friendship and confidence, and probably never loves you so vividly as in these still moments. No matter that twilight is falling, and that you cannot see each other's faces, the presence and the silence are full of brightness and eloquence, and you feel they are enough.

Even so we may be silent to the Lord. Just because we know He loves us so really and understands us so thoroughly! There is no need when very weary, bodily or mentally, or both, to force ourselves to entertain Him, so to speak; to go through a sort of duty-work of a certain amount of uttered words or arranged thoughts. That might be if He were only to us as a wayfaring man that turneth aside to tarry for a night, but not with the beloved and Gracious One who has come in to abide with us, and is always there! If this is His relation to us, there is no fear but what there will be, at other times, plenty of intercourse; but now, when we are "so tired," we may just be silent to Him, instead of speaking to Him.

This is one of the expressions which are exclusively used concerning the things of God. There is no such thing as being silent to anyone else. Silent *with* a mortal friend, but never silent *to* any but the Immortal One. Though it has its earthly analogy, it is not identically the same. For none but our Lord can interpret the unseen pulsings of that which to human ken is *only* silence. He hears the music they are measuring out before Him. He takes the confidence of that hush at its full value of golden love. He sees the soul's attitude of devotion and faith through the shadows which hide it from itself.

Sometimes He takes the opportunity of our silence to speak Himself. He answers it "with good words and comfortable words." And do we not know that one such word from Him is more than anything else, worth ten thousandfold all the weariness or exhaustion of pain which brought us to be silent!

But sometimes He answers silence with silence. What then? Are we to conclude that He is gone away, or is not thinking about us, forgetting to be gracious? We are judging Him as He would not judge us. He did not put such an interpretation on our silence; then why should we on His? Let us take His interpretation of it; surely we should believe what He Himself asserts! "He will be silent in His love" (Zephaniah 3:17, *margin*). Can any words be more beautiful! It is as if He, even He, who made man's mouth, had made no words which could express His exceeding great love, and therefore He could only expand it in the silence which lies above and below and beyond all language. When we have said, as very likely we have often done, "Why art Thou silent unto me, O Lord?" why did we not take His own exquisite answer, and trust the love that was veiled in the silence? For whenever we can say, "Truly my soul wait-eth upon (Hebrew: "is silent to") God," we may rest assured that any appar-ent waiting on His part is only "that He may be gracious," yes, "*very* gracious unto thee."

We may be sure He has many things to say to us, when He sees we can bear them. But till His time to speak is come, let our silence of trust respond to His silence of love.

This sonnet by F.R.H., not published in *Starlight Through the Shadows*, was pub-lished in her first book, *The Ministry of Song*, and is added here at the end of Chapter III.

Silent in Love.

"He will rest [1] in his love." ZEPHANIAH 3:17.

LOVE culminates in bliss when it doth reach
  A white, unflickering, fear-consuming glow;
  And, knowing it is known as it doth know,
Needs no assuring word or soothing speech.
It craves but silent nearness, so to rest,
  No sound, no movement, love not heard but felt,
  Longer and longer still, till time should melt,
A snow-flake on the eternal ocean's breast.

  Have moments of this silence starred thy past,
Made memory a glory-haunted place,
Taught all the joy that mortal ken can trace?
  By greater light 'tis but a shadow cast;—
So shall the Lord thy God rejoice o'er thee,
And in His love will rest, and silent be.

[1] Marginal reading—"*be silent.*"

CHAPTER IV.

The Dew of the Word.

"My speech shall distil as the dew."—DEUTERONOMY 32:2.

B UT who hears the dew fall? What microphone could reveal that music to our "gross unpurgèd ears"?

The dew distils in silence. So does the speech of our God. Most frequently in the silence of trust already spoken of. In that stillness God's silent love can be condensed into dewlike communications; not read, not heard, but made known by the direct power of the Spirit upon the soul.

Most often He does this by thrilling into remembrance something from the written Word, already learnt, but now flashing out in the quickened memory as if it had never been heard before.

We do not get much of this if we are always in the midst of noise and turmoil and bustle. He can, and now and then He does, send this "speech" through a very chaos of bustle or trouble. He can make a point of silence in the very centre of a cyclone, and speak there to our hearts. But the more usual way is to make a wider silence for His dew to fall, by calling us apart into some quiet place of sorrow or sickness. So when we find ourselves thus led into a wilderness, let us forthwith look out for the dew, and it will not fail. Then our desert will rejoice and blossom as the rose; very likely much more so than the hot harvestfields, or the neat gardens from which we have been called away.

The dew distils in darkness. Not in the darkness of external trial alone, it is easy to understand that, and most of us have experienced it. The beautiful thing is that the life-giving speech distils even in soul darkness. "Who is among you that feareth the Lord, that walketh in darkness and hath no light? Let him trust in the name of the Lord, and stay himself upon his God." There are times when we simply cannot see anything, when there is nothing for it but to hold on and trust in the dark; times when we do not seem even to be walking in the dark, but when, like Micah, we "*sit* in darkness," too feeble even to grope. Such darkness often comes in a time of reaction and weariness after special work and exertion, very often indeed after great or exciting success, sometimes even after unusually vivid spiritual blessing. An interval of convalescence after acute illness, when the overtaxed nervous energy has more than it can do in slowly refilling the chalice of life that had been so nearly "spilled on the ground," is peculiarly liable to it. And the sufferers who never pass beyond that stage, who are never any more than "a *little* better," know its shadow perhaps best of all. It does not say so, but I think the Lord Jesus must have known it, because He was made like unto us in all things, and submitted not only to the causes but to the effects of all the natural experiences of the nature which He took on Him.

Now it seems to me that it is in this kind of darkness that His speech distils as the dew. You look out some dark night after a hot dusty day; there is no storm, no rain, there is not the least token to your senses of what is going on. You look out again in the morning, and you see every blade and leaf tipped with a dewdrop; everything is revived and freshened, prepared for the heat of the day, and smiling at the glow. Just so His words are silently falling on your souls in the darkness, and preparing them for the day. They do not come with any sensible power, nothing flashes out from the page as at other times, nothing shines so as to shed any pleasant light on your path, you do not hear any sound of abundance of rain. You seem as if you could not take the words in; and if you could, your mind is too weary to meditate on them. But they are distilling as the dew all the time!

Do not quarrel with the invisible dew because it is not a visible shower. The Lord would send a shower if that was the true need to be supplied to His vineyard; but as He is sending His speech in another form, you may be quite sure it is because He is supplying your true need thereby. You cannot see why it is so, and I do not pretend to explain; but what does that matter! He knows which way to water His vineyard. These words of His, which you are remembering so feebly, or reading without being able to grasp, are not going to return void. They are doing His own work on your soul, only in a quite different way to what you would choose. By and by they will sparkle out in the light of a new morning, and you will find yourself starting fresh, and perhaps wondering how it is that the leaves of life which hung so limp and drooping are so fresh and firm again on their stems. This also cometh forth from the Lord of hosts, which is wonderful in counsel, and excellent in working.

The dew falls not in one mass of water, but innumerable little drops. What one drop does not reach another does. So it is not one overwhelmingly powerful word which does this holy night work in the soul, but the unrealized influence of many, dropping softly on the plants of the Lord which He has planted, one resting here, another there; one touching an unrecognised need, and another reaching an unconsciously failing grace. "Each drop uncounted hath its own mission, and is duly sent to its own leaf or blade."

Sometimes God's dew goes on falling through many hours of the night. The watches seem very long, and the starlight does not reveal it. But none of it is lost; some is already doing a hidden work as it falls around the very roots of our being, and some is ready to be revealed in sparkling brightness when the night is over, lessons learnt among the shadows to be lived out in the sunshine.

The object of the dew is to maintain life in dry places and seasons. Dwellers in rainless regions understand this better than we do, but we can see enough of it in any dry week in summer to understand the beauty of the figure. So this speech is spirit and life to souls which are, however feebly, yet really alive unto God. Dew does nothing for the stones. You would not know there ever was any at all if you only look at the gravel path. And it makes no difference at all to a dead leaf. But if it falls on the little fading plant that could hardly have lived through many more days of July sunshine, the weak little stem straightens up as the leaves absorb the life-renewing moisture, and the closed blossom can open out again with fresher fragrance than before. So God keeps on distilling His speech into our frail spiritual life, or it would soon wither up. Dryness is more to be dreaded than darkness.

Only let us be trustfully content to let this dew of heaven fall in the dark, and when we cannot hear or see, recollect that He says, "My speech shall distil as the dew." Our part is to believe this, and leave ourselves open to it as we read what perhaps seems a very dim page of the Bible with very tired eyes; or, perhaps, lie still through the long hours of a literal night, with no power to meditate on the fitful gleams of half recollected verses that just cross our minds and seem to leave no trace. Never mind, the dew is falling!

> Softly the dew in the evening descends,
>   Cooling the sun-heated ground and the gale;
> Flow'rets all fainting it soothingly tends,
>   Ere the consumings of mid-day prevail.
> Sweet gentle dewdrops, how mystic your fall,
> Wisdom and mercy float down in you all.
>
> Softer and sweeter by far is that Dew
>   Which from the Fountain of Comfort distils,
> When the worn heart is created anew,
>   And hallowed pleasure its emptiness fills.
> Lord, let Thy Spirit be-dew my dry fleece!
> Faith then shall triumph, and trouble shall cease.
>
> *(Rev. W. H. Havergal: last hymn,* 1870.)

CHAPTER V.

With Whom We Have to Do.

"Him with whom we have to do."—HEBREWS 4:13.

THERE are wonderful depths of comfort in these words. I cannot fathom them for you. I only want to guide you to look where the deep places are, asking the Holy Spirit to put a long sounding line into your hand, that you may prove for yourself how great is the depth.

These words seem to meet every sort of need of comfort. If it is perplexity, or oppressive puzzle what to do, when we cannot see through things;—or if it is being unable to explain yourself to others, and trials or complications arising out of this: just fall back upon "Him with whom we have to do," to whose eyes all things are naked and opened. He is your Guide,—why need you puzzle? He is your Shield,—why need you try so hard or wish so much to explain and vindicate yourself?

If it is sense of *sin* which does not let you be comfortable, turn *at once* to "Him with whom you have to do." Remember, it is not with Satan that you have to do, nor with your accusing conscience, but with Jesus. He will deal with all the rest; you only have to deal with Him. And He is your great High Priest. He has made full Atonement for you; for the very sins that are weighing on you now. The blood of that Atonement, His own precious blood, cleanseth us from all sin. Cleanseth whom? People that have not sinned? People that don't want to be cleansed? Thank God for the word "cleanseth *us*," us who have sinned and who want to be cleansed. And you have to do with Him who shed it for your cleansing, who His own self bare your sins in His own body on the tree.

If it is *temptation* that will not let you rest, come straight away out of the very thick of it; it may be with the fiery darts sticking in you. Come with all the haunting thoughts that you hate, just as you are, to "Him with whom you have to do." You would not or could not tell the temptations to any one else; but then you have not got to do with any one else in the matter, but *only* with Jesus. And He "suffered, being tempted." The very fact that you are distressed by the temptation proves that it *is* temptation, and that you have a singular claim on the sympathy of our tempted Lord, a claim which He most tenderly acknowledges. But use it instantly; don't creep, but flee unto Him to hide you from the assaults which you are too weak to meet.

If it is *bodily weakness, sickness, or pain*, how very sweet it is to know that we have to do with Jesus, who is "touched with the feeling of our infirmities." (The word is the same that is elsewhere translated sickness: John 11:2–4.) Don't you sometimes find it very hard to make even your doctor understand *what* the pain is like? Words don't seem to convey it. And after you have explained the trying and wearying sensation as best you can, you are convinced those who have not felt it do not understand it.

Now think of Jesus not merely entering into the fact, but into the feeling, of what you are going through. "Touched with the *feeling*"—how deep that goes! When we turn away to Him in our wordless weariness of pain which *only* He understands, we find out that we have to do with Him in quite a different sense from how we have to do with any one else. We could not do without Him, and thank God we shall never have to do without Him.

Why enumerate other shadows which this same soft light can enter and dispel? They may be cast by any imaginable or unimaginable shape of trouble or need, but the same light rises for them all, if we will only turn towards the brightness of its rising. For Jesus is He "with whom we have to do" in *every thing*, nothing can be outside of this, unless we wilfully decline to have to do with Him in it, or unbelievingly choose to have to do with "lords many."

And we are answerable only to Him in every thing; for this is included in having to do with Him. To our own Master we stand or fall; and that latter alternative is instantly put out of the question, the apostle adding, "Yea, he shall be holden up, for God is able to make him stand," *i.e.,* he who is his "own Master's" servant. To Him we have to give account, if from Him we take our orders.

We have to do with Him *directly*. So directly that it is difficult at first to grasp the directness. There is absolutely nothing between the soul and Jesus, if we will but have it so. We have Himself as our Mediator with God, and the very characteristic of a mediator is, as Job says, "that he might lay his hand upon us both"; so the hand of Jesus, who is Himself "the Man of Thy right hand," is laid upon us with no intermediate link and no intervening distance. We do not need any paper and print, let alone any human voice, between us and Himself.

"To Thee, O dear, dear Saviour,
My spirit turns for rest."

That turning is instinctive and instantaneous when we have once learnt what it is to have direct and personal dealing with the Lord Jesus Christ. Life is altogether a different thing then, whether shady or sunshiny, and a stranger intermeddleth not with our hidden joy. Perhaps it is just this that makes such a strangely felt difference between those who equally profess and call themselves Christians. Is Jesus to us *Him with whom we have to do*? or is He only Him whom we know about, and believe about, and with whose laws and ordinances we have to do? This makes all the difference, and every one who has this personal dealing with Him *knows* it, and cannot help knowing it.

Do not let this discourage any one who cannot yet say *"Him with whom I have to do."* For He is more ready and willing thus to have to do with you, than you with Him. You may enter at once into this most sweet and solemn position. He is there already: He only waits for you to come into it. Only bring Him your sins and your sinful self, "waiting not to rid your soul of one dark blot." Nothing else separates between you and Him, and He will take them all away and receive you graciously; and then you too shall know the sacred and secret blessedness of having to do with Jesus.

I could not do without Thee,
    O Jesus, Saviour dear!
E'en when my eyes are holden,
    I know that Thou art near.
How dreary and how lonely
    This changeful life would be,
Without the sweet communion,
    The secret rest with Thee.

I could not do without Thee!
    No other friend can read
The spirit's strange deep longings,
    Interpreting its need.
No human heart could enter
    Each deep recess of mine,
And soothe and hush and calm it,
    O blessèd Lord, but Thine!

CHAPTER VI.

Things Which He Suffered.

"The things which He suffered."—Hebrews 5:8.

I F we have some dear one gone before, who "suffered many things," there is neither comfort nor help to be had by dwelling on them. It would be a poor comforter who reminded you of them, and brought them back in detail to your scarred memory. One would rather do one's utmost to turn your thoughts away from them, leading you to dwell only on the present bliss, and one would fain blot out your painful remembrance of a past which it does no good to recall.

Not so does our Divine Comforter work. When He takes of the things of Christ and shows them to us, we feel that the things which He suffered are precious exceedingly, and the Spirit-wrought remembrance of them powerful beyond all else.

These "things" are only past in act, not in effect. For He was wounded for our transgressions and bruised for our iniquities of this day; the chastisement of the peace of this hour was upon Him; and though the whole head may be sick and the whole heart faint, the stripes that fell on Him are full of fresh power to heal at this moment.

> "Thy sin of *this* day
> In its shadow lay
> Between My face and One turned away."

Greater love hath no man than this, that a man lay down his life for his friends; yet that was only one of the things which He suffered, only the full stop at the close of the great charter of suffering love.

This pathetic plural is full of suggestion. How much suffering is dimly hinted in the one intimation that He bare our sicknesses! How much may be hidden under the supposition of the Jews that He was nearly fifty years of age, when so little beyond thirty! How sharp must have been the experiences which graved such lines upon the visage so marred more than any man! Think of all that must have gone on under the surface of His home life, where neither did His brethren believe in Him. Consider Him that endured such contradiction of sinners against Himself. Think what temptation must have been to the Holy One, and what the concentration of malice and great rage when the prince of darkness went forth to do his worst against the lonely Son of Man, whom he knew to be the Son of God. Think of Jesus *alone* with Satan! Oh, what things He suffered *before* He came to the agony and bloody sweat, the cross and passion, which filled up the cup which His Father gave Him to drink for us men and for our salvation!

All this true! all this real! all this for us!

All this, that He might be made a perfect Saviour, having learnt by personal experience the suffering from which He saves as well as the suffering in which He supports and with which He sympathises; having learnt by personal experience the obedience by which " many shall be made righteous," and which is at once our justification and our example.

All this, that He might be a perfect Captain of our salvation, knowing all and far more than all the hardships of the rank and file.

All this, that He might be the Author of eternal salvation to them that obey Him, to you and me!

"The things which He suffered." The remembrance must touch our gratitude and love, if anything will. If when we looked back on some terrible suffering unto death of one who loved us dearly, suppose an elder brother, I really do not know how any heart could bear it, if we distinctly knew that all that prolonged agony was borne instead of us, and borne for nothing in the world but for love of us. But if to this were added the knowledge that we had behaved abominably to that dying brother, done all sorts of things, now beyond recall, to grieve and vex him, not cared one bit about his love or made him any return of even natural affection, held aloof from him and sided with those who were against him; and *then* the terrible details of his slow agony were told, nay *shown* to us,—well, imagine our remorse if you can, I cannot! The burden of grief and gratitude would be crushing, and if there were still any possible way in which we could show that poor, late gratitude, we should take it at any cost, or rather, we should count nothing at any cost if we might but prove our tardy love. Only I think we should never know another hour's rest. But it is part of the strange power of the remembrance of our Lord's sufferings that it brings strength and solace and peace; for, as Bunyan says, "He hath given us rest by His sorrow." The bitterness of death to Him is the very fountain of the sweetness of life to us. Do the words after all seem to fall without power or reality on your heart? Is it nothing, or very little more than nothing, to you? Not that you do not know it is all true, but your heart seems cold, and your apprehension mechanical, and your faith paralysed;—does this describe you? Thank God that feelings do not alter facts! He suffered for this sinful coldness as well as for all other sins. He suffered, the Just for the unjust; and are we not emphatically unjust when we requite His tremendous love this way? Still you don't feel it, though you own it. You see it all, but it is through a transparent wall of ice. What is to be done? Ask, and ask at once, for the Holy Spirit, that He may melt the ice and take of these things of Christ, showing them to you, not in the light of natural understanding and mere mental reception of undeniable facts, but revealing them with His own Divine power and bowing your whole soul under the weight of the exceeding great love of our Master and only Saviour Jesus Christ, as manifested in " the things which He suffered." " For every one that asketh receiveth."

CHAPTER VII.

The Lord's Cherishing.

"Cherisheth it."—Ephesians 5:29.

"CHERISHETH it, even as the Lord the church." The church is not only "one body," but also "many members"; "for the body is not one member, but many." And what is true for the whole is true also for the smallest part. Lest any one should think the individual is rather lost in the great whole, the gracious word of our God comes down to meet the possible or passing tremor, and says: "Ye are," not only the body of Christ, but "members in particular."

Do not hesitate to take all the revelation of love that shines softly through this one word "cherisheth," for your own self; for the more you feel yourself to be the weakest imaginable member of Christ, unworthy to be a member at all of His glorious body, the more closely and sweetly will it apply to you.

For it necessarily implies, on the one side, weakness and inferiority and need. It would be nothing to us if we felt extremely strong and capable and self-contained. The Lord would never have taken the trouble to cause it to be written for such people. They would neither want it nor thank Him for it. We do not talk about "cherishing" an oak tree, or an athlete, or even a "strong minded woman." Our heart-welcome to this beautiful word, and our sense of its preciousness, will be just in proportion to our sense of being among the Lord's little ones, or weak ones, no matter what others suppose us to be. After all, are not even those who are chasing thousands, but little ones? and those who are slaying Goliaths, but weak ones? in their real and hidden relationship to their own great and mighty Saviour and Lord. Even a father in Christ or a mother in Israel may turn with the heart of a little child, lovingly and gratefully, and perhaps very wearily too, to their cherishing Lord, to be comforted afresh with the old comforts, and hushed to rest on the little pillow of some very familiar text.

The Lord Jesus has said of all who love Him, "I will love him and will manifest Myself to him." See how He manifested Himself to you in these words, as your Cherisher. The word conveys, on His side, nothing but affection, and gentle thoughtful care. How do we cherish a little weak plant? There were plenty of handsomer ones, but this little cutting or seedling was perhaps a gift in the first place; and then we took a fancy to it, so that we cared doubly for it. Then we felt a sort of pity for it, because it was such a delicate little thing; so we shielded it, and perhaps re-potted it, that it might strike its little roots more freely. We watched it day by day, giving it just enough water and not too much. We set it in the light when it was ready, and turned it round now and then, so that even too much light might not make it grow one-sidedly. And when at last it put out a flower for us, we thought more of that than of any ninety-nine blossoms in the great garden. Is not this something like our Lord's cherishing?

Then think how "a nurse cherisheth her children." (1 Thessalonians 2:7.) That is, a "gentle" and wise one. How the little ailments are watched and attended to; how the little weary heads are laid on her shoulders and stroked to sleep; how the little meals are regulated and given; *never* forgotten,—who ever heard of such a thing! How the little garments are kept clean and comfortable, changed and mended, as need may be. How the nursery fire is looked after (while all the while the guard is kept on the bars), so that the room should not be too hot or too cold. How the little bodies are cared for and loved every inch, even the little fingers and toes! How the little fancies are borne with and entered into, not unheeded or scorned; and the silly little questions patiently answered, and the baby lessons taught, and the small tempers managed, and checked, and forgiven! That is cherishing. Need we trace its close resemblance to the dealings of our infinitely patient and gentle Lord?

Then think of the still higher and closer cherishing of the weak wife by the strong husband,—itself shown by the only possible stronger figure, "No man ever yet hated *his own flesh*, but nourisheth and cherisheth it"; this set forth by the Holy Ghost through the pen of an apostle, to convey to *you* some dim idea of the Lord's love and care and thought for *you*. What could He say more? For even thus the Lord cherisheth you,—He gives you His name to bear as your honour, and His very heart to dwell in as the home of your soul. He gives you the right of constant access, the right of continual dwelling in His presence. He makes you partaker of His very nature, joining you unto Himself, not only in a perpetual covenant, but as "one spirit" with Him. He pays all your debts, and now all your wants lie upon Him, and these wants are each and all foreseen and provided for, and supplied with untiring love. He knows in an instant when you are weary or ailing, whether in body or spirit, and knows how to speak the right word for either, speaking verily to your heart,—knows, too, when to be silent for a little while. His cherishing goes on night and day,—just as much in the dark as in the light; and will go on, faithfully, ceaselessly, all through your life-long need of it, unto the end; and there is no shadowing whisper to fall upon this life-long manifestation of love, no such word as "till death us do part." No absence of your Lord shall deprive you of it; and all that death can do is to take away the last veil, that you may see face to face, and know even as you are known. His care over you will then be exchanged for perfect joy over you. "He shall see of the travail of His soul and be satisfied."

> "From glory unto glory." Though tribulation fall,
> It cannot touch our treasure when Christ is all in all!
> Whatever lies before us, there can be nought to fear,
> For what are pain and sorrow *when Jesus Christ is near?*

CHAPTER VIII.

Fresh Glory.

"My glory was fresh in me."—Job 29:20.

WHO does not know the longing for freshness? Fresh air, fresh water, fresh flowers, the freshness of children, and of some people's conversation and writings,—all illustrate or lead up to that spiritual freshness which is both pleasure and power. For it was when Job's glory was fresh in him, that his bow was renewed in his hand. Freshness and glory! and yet the brilliant music of such words is brought down to a minor strain by one little touch—it " *was*," not " *it is*"; a melancholy Past instead of a bright Present. Now, instead of saddening ourselves unnecessarily by sighing, "Ah, yes! that is always the way," let us see how we may personally prove that it is not always the way, and that Job's confessedly exceptional experience need not, and ought not, to be ours.

First of all, if our glory is to be fresh in us, it all depends upon what the glory in us is. If it is any sort of our own—anything connected with that which decayeth and waxeth old in us or passeth away around us—of course it cannot be always fresh, any more than the freshness of dawn or of springtime can last. Neither material nor mental states can retain their exquisite and subtle charm, and spiritual states are no better off; "frames and feelings" have an inherent tendency to subside into flatness, dulness, staleness, or whatever else expresses the want of freshness. There is only one unfailing source of unfailing freshness— Christ Himself. "Thou hast the dew of Thy youth"—the only dew that never dries up through any heat or dust. "Christ in you, the hope of glory." His word is, "For her." Your word should be, "Thou, O Lord, art my glory." I know it seems a great thing to claim, but the indwelling of Christ is not something reserved for only a few very exalted saints. The words are very plain: "Know ye not your own selves, how that Jesus Christ is in you, except ye be reprobates?" Take it just as you see it there. Jesus Christ is in you, if you have opened the door of your heart to let Him come in. He is "in you the hope of glory," if you have admitted Him; and He *is* your glory. If so, you may sing, "My glory *is* fresh in me," and never fear a change to Job's minor! He had but a prophetic glimpse, through shadowing centuries, of a Redeemer yet to come; you have the full view of the fact of His finished work, and His promised, and therefore present, presence all the days; so this mournful experience only proves how different yours is meant to be.

Jesus Christ is *always* fresh.

Don't we know it? Do we not always find Him so, when we are in direct personal communication with Him, with "nothing between"? Are we not conscious that when we lament over want of freshness, it really means want of Jesus? We go and bemoan about it to a friend perhaps, and ask what to do; and all the while, down at the bottom, we are secretly aware that they can do nothing more or better than advise us to "go and tell Jesus"—to get into direct personal contact with Him, alone with Him, again! The very same time we spent, in this sort of second-hand cistern-seeking, would be far more resultful if spent in re-opening communion with Him, and drawing from the Fountain itself. That is always open. "All my fresh springs are in Thee," not in our kind Christian friends.

All that we receive from Jesus is *always* fresh. How fresh His most familiar words come, when He gives them to us by His Spirit! What is ever fresher than the old, old story, when any part of it is heard with the ear of faith? and our response is "Jesus died for *me!*" What is ever fresher, whether in outward sacramental act, or in the thousand times repeated heart communion which waits not for time and place, than the remembrance of the exceeding great love of our Master and only Saviour, with its appropriating echo, "Jesus loves *me!*" The water that we draw out of these wells of salvation is always fresh indeed. And so is the manna on which He would have us feed continually.

And so is the oil with which He anoints us. There is the great first anointing to be His kings and priests, wherewith He "*hath* anointed us" (2 Corinthians 1:21). Then comes the present, "Thou anointest my head with oil," as His received and honoured guests, sinners though we be, when the table is prepared, and the cup runneth over, and we realize our new position as partakers of His grace. But then comes, "I *shall be* anointed with *fresh* oil!" A beautiful Future for all the days of our life; the always fresh anointings, the continual "*supply* of the Spirit of Jesus Christ." Fresh oil of joy in the midst of the mourning through which we may pass, fresh oil of gladness in fellowship with our holy King (Psalm 45:7), fresh oil of consecration as day by day is given up to Him who has redeemed our lives, fresh oil upon the sacrifice as we offer our " praise to God continually, that is, the fruit of our lips."

Fresh springs, fresh oil, fresh glory!

With such resources, ought we to feel dusty? Is not the fault in ourselves? And if so, what is to hinder us from coming at once to the Triune source of all blessed renewal and freshness? It is Jesus our Saviour who is the ever fresh glory within us. It is the Holy Spirit, our Comforter, who shall pour His fresh oil upon us. With such resources, ought we not to refresh those around us? Ought they not to take knowledge of us that we have such a well of water within us, springing up into everlasting life? Ought there not to be a dewy fragrance in our lives, in our words and ways, that may silently witness to the reality of the source of our freshness? It is one of our special privileges to do this.

CHAPTER IX.

This God Is Our God.

"This God is our God."—Psalm 48:14.

WHEN once we have obeyed the beseeching command, "Be ye reconciled to God," and, being justified by faith, have peace with God through our Lord Jesus Christ, we have a right as His reconciled children to take the strong consolation of these words. They are then a seal of appropriation upon the whole revelation.

Every part of God's word is a revelation, more or less clear, of Himself. When we do not see this, it is only that we miss it, not that it is not there. Do we not know how very possible it is to read the historical parts merely *as* history, and the prophetical merely as prophecy, and the doctrinal merely as doctrine, and miss the vision of God which everywhere shines through the glass darkly, if only His good Spirit opens our eyes to see it! And even when we do trace out God Himself in His recorded works and ways, how often we miss the personal comfort of remembering our own close and personal interest in what we see of His character and attributes. It makes all the difference to recollect, at every glimpse of these, that "*this* God is *our* God!"

It is wonderful what a freshness and reality the simple application of this little verse will give to all our reading. Just try it at once, whatever may be the next passage you read! I question if there is a single chapter, from the first of Genesis to the twenty-second of Revelation, which will not reflect the light of this beautiful little lamp. First ask for the direct and present and fresh anointing of the Holy Spirit, that you may behold your God. And then, whether your gaze is turned upon a promise which reveals Him as the Loving One, or a warning which reveals Him as the Just and Holy One; whether you read a history which shows His grand grasp in ordering the centuries, or a verse which shows His delicate touch upon the turn of a moment—as you admire, say, "*This* God is our

God." When you read "Great things doeth He which we cannot comprehend," and the splendid variety of His book gives a glimpse of His power and glory in upholding the things which are seen, from the hosts of million-aged stars to the fleeting flakes of the "treasures of the snow," say, "*This* God is our God."

When you come to the many direct and gracious declarations of what God is, you will find these words light them up splendidly. "The Lord, the Lord God, gracious and merciful, longsuffering, and abundant in goodness and truth." *This* God is our God! "The Lord is good, a stronghold in the day of trouble." *This* God is our God! "*Glorious* in holiness, fearful in praises, doing wonders." *This* God is our God! "God is love." *This* God is our God!

When you come to those parts of the Bible which are too often under-valued and left out of the daily reading, still, though it may be through a less transparent veil, God will reveal Himself. For instance, when you come to the genealogies in Chronicles, consider how His individual care is illustrated by the otherwise unknown names, noted in His book because of their connection with Christ; no matter how remote that connection, through the distant gen-erations and collateral branches, might seem to human ways of thinking. And then remember that "this God," Who thus inscribed their individual names for Christ's sake, is "our God" who has inscribed our individual names in the book of life for Christ's sake, because we are chosen in Him. And when we read the life of His dear Son, and see what that beloved Son, in the infinite loveableness of His exquisite perfection, must have been to the Father who yet spared Him not; and, most of all, when we read of the hand of God being laid upon the Man of His right hand, when He made the iniquities of us all to meet on Him, and let Him suffer unto death for us men and for our salvation, then, above all, let us turn to God the Father and say, "This God, who *so* loved the world, is *our* God!"

It seems as if this personal relationship to us as our "God," were one in which He specially delights, and which He would have us keep continually in mind. In Deuteronomy, that wonderful book of reminders, He has caused this gracious name, "the Lord thy God," or "the Lord your God," to be writ-ten no less than two hundred and twenty-seven times. What a name for Him to be revealed by to the wayward wanderers of Israel! and what comfort to us that He is the same God to us! When you want a helpful Bible subject to work out, suppose you take this, and trace out all through the Bible under what cir-cumstances or with what context of precious teaching He gives these words, and let the gladness of the search be "This God is *our* God." And then trace out (with your concordance if you like,) the responses to this constantly repeated and heart-strengthening Name, noting and arranging the passages that speak of

"Our God." Between these you will find every soul need for time and eternity supplied, from the first great need of the awakened sinner who is met with the words "He that is our God is the God of salvation," to the fulness of present blessing, "God, even our own God, shall bless us," and the fulness of future joy when "thy God (shall be) thy glory."

As you study, the claim will grow closer, and the response will intensify from the wide chorus of "Our God" to the fervent thrill of the whisper, "O God, Thou art *my* God."

Some of us may have an unexpressed notion that, after all, this does not come so near to us as the thought of "Jesus, my Saviour." We almost feel dazzled at the vastness of the idea of "God." And we take refuge, mentally, in what seems more within reach. This is almost always the case in the earlier stages of our Christian life. Having been drawn by the Father to the Lord Jesus Christ, we almost lose sight of the Father in the Son, instead of beholding the glory of God in the face of Jesus Christ as He intends us to do. Practically, some of us know consciously only one Person in the Blessed Trinity, and do not honour the Father as we honour the Son. If so, let us ask the Holy Spirit to lead us on into all truth, and to mature our spiritual powers and widen our spiritual vision that we may know more of what God means when He reveals Himself, not only by some name which human relationships enable us to grasp, but as our *God*.

We shall not love Jesus less, but more, as we learn to love God, who was in Christ reconciling us to Himself. We shall not be less tenderly grateful for His coming to die for us, but more as we rise to adore the mystery of love which alone illumines the inconceivable eternity of the past when the Word was with God and the Word was God.

We shall find, too, that, while there is more than scope enough in the thought and revelation of God *as* God for the strongest hour, the very zenith of our intellect, there is rest in it for the weariest hour of the weakest frame. For when my heart and my flesh faileth, God is the strength of my heart and my portion for ever. And this God *is* our God for ever and ever. He will be our guide *even unto death*.

For the sad and sinful
　　Shall His grace abound;
For the faint and feeble
　　Perfect strength be found.
I, the Lord, am with thee,
　　Be thou not afraid!

I will help and strengthen,
　　Be thou not dismayed!
Yea, I will uphold thee
　　With My own Right Hand,
Thou art called and chosen
　　In My sight to stand.

" SATISFIED."

" He shall see of the travail of his soul, and shall be satisfied."—Isa. liii. 11.

REJOICE with Jesus Christ to-day,	Lu. xv. 6.
All ye who love His holy sway !	Ps. cx. 3.
The travail of His soul is past,	Isa. liii. 11.
He shall be satisfied at last.	Isa. xlix. 7, 8.
Rejoice with Him, rejoice indeed,	John iii. 29.
For He shall see His chosen seed !	Isa. liii. 10.
But ours the trust, the grand employ,	1 Cor. iii. 9.
To work out this divinest joy.	Zeph. iii. 17-20.
Of all His own He loseth none,	John xvii. 12.
They shall be gathered one by one ;	Isa. xxvii. 12.
He garnereth the smallest grain,	Amos ix. 9.
His travail shall not be in vain !	Heb. ii. 13.
Arise, and work ! arise, and pray	2 Pet. iii. 12.
That He would haste the dawning day !	Cant. ii. 18.
And let the silver trumpet sound,	Lev. xxv. 9, 10.
Wherever Satan's slaves are found.	Isa. lxi. 1.
The vanquished foe shall soon be stilled,	Ps. viii. 2.
The conquering Saviour's joy fulfilled—	Jude 24.
Fulfilled in us, fulfilled in them—	John xvii. 13.
His crown, His royal diadem.	Isa. lxii. 3.
Soon, soon our waiting eyes shall see	Matt. xxvi. 64.
The Saviour's mighty Jubilee !	1 Thess. i. 10.
His harvest joy is filling fast ;	Isa. ix. 3, *marg.*
He shall be satisfied at last.	Ps. cxxvi. 6.

FRANCES RIDLEY HAVERGAL.

references by
F. R. H. this old copy
from her study.

This leaflet poem was found among Havergal manuscripts and papers. The note at the bottom was written likely by her sister, Maria: references by F.R.H. This <u>old</u> copy from her study.

CHAPTER X.

Thy Hand.

"Thy hand presseth me sore."—PSALM 38:2.

WHEN the pressure is sorest, the hand must be nearest. What should we do in suffering if we were left to imagine that it was Satan's hand that presses so sore! Our Father has not left us in any doubt about it. This settles it: "Thy hand"; "Thou didst it"(Psalm 39:9); "It is the blow of Thine hand" (Psalm 39:10); "Thy hand was heavy upon me" (Psalm 32:4). It cannot be otherwise, for "in the shadow of His hand hath He hid you" (Isaiah 49:2); and how can any other press you there? What is hid in God's hand must be out of reach of Satan's.

The hand is the most sensitive member, gifted with the most quick and delicate nerves of touch. When it presses, it instinctively measures the pressure; the contact is the closest possible; the throb which cannot be seen is felt, truly and immediately. This is how His dear hand is pressing you; this is what the pain means.

Have you ever watched the exceedingly delicate and yet firm pressure of the hand of a skilful tuner? He will make the string produce a perfectly true note, vibrating in absolute accord with his own never changing tuning-fork. The practised hand is at one with the accurate ear, and the pressure is brought to bear with most delicate adjustment to the resistance: the tension is never exceeded, he never breaks a string; but he patiently strikes the note again and again, till the tone is true and his ear is satisfied, and then the muscles relax and the pressure ceases. The string may be a poor little thin one, yielding a very small note; but that does not matter at all; it is wanted in its place: just as much as a great bass one, that can yield a volume of deep sound. The tuner takes just the same pains with it, and is just satisfied when it vibrates true to the pitch, retaining its own individual tone. That string could not tune itself, and no machine was ever invented to accomplish it; nothing but the firm and sensitive pressure of the tuner's own living hand can bring it into tune.

Will you not trust your Tuner, and begin a note of praise even under the pressure?

> "Yet take Thy way; for sure Thy way is best
> Stretch or contract me, Thy poor debtor.
> This is but tuning of my breast,
> To make the music better."
>
> GEORGE HERBERT.

A Song in the Night.

I take this pain, Lord Jesus,
　　From Thine own hand;
The strength to bear it bravely
　　Thou wilt command.
I am too weak for effort,
　　So let me rest,
In hush of sweet submission,
　　On Thine own breast.

I take this pain, Lord Jesus,
　　As proof indeed
That Thou art watching closely
　　My truest need:
That Thou my Good Physician,
　　Art watching still;
That all Thine own good pleasure
　　Thou wilt fulfill.

I take this pain, Lord Jesus!
　　What Thou dost choose
The soul that really loves Thee
　　Will not refuse:
It is not for the first time
　　I trust today;

For Thee my heart has never
　　A trustless "Nay!"

I take this pain, Lord Jesus!
　　But what beside?
'Tis no unmingled portion
　　Thou dost provide.
In every hour of faintness,
　　My cup runs o'er
With faithfulness and mercy
　　And love's sweet store.

I take this pain, Lord Jesus,
　　As Thine own gift,
And *true* though tremulous praises
　　I now uplift;
I am too weak to sing them,
　　But Thou dost hear
The whisper from the pillow—
　　Thou art so near!

'Tis Thy dear hand, O Saviour,
　　That presseth sore,
The hand that bears the nail-prints
　　For evermore.
And now beneath its shadow,
　　Hidden by Thee,
The *pressure* only tells me
　　Thou lovest me!

CHAPTER XI.

I Pray for Them.

"I pray for them."—JOHN 17:9.

H E ever liveth to make intercession for us; and so while you have been silent to Him, He has been praying for you. If His hand has been upon you so that you could not pray, why need you be mourning over this, when your merciful and faithful High Priest has been offering up the pure and sweet and costly incense of His own intercession? But if your heart condemns you, and you know you gave way to indolent coldness when you might have roused yourself to more prayer, will it not touch you to recollect that, in His wonderful long-suffering, Jesus has been praying instead!

What confident and powerful petitions for His disciples He was pouring out when He said, "I pray for them." And how gracious of Him to let us overhear such breathings of Almighty love on their behalf. If He had said no more than this, we might have tremulously inferred that, being always the same Lord, He might give us a remote share of some reflected blessing from this prayer. But He anticipates a wish that we should hardly have been bold enough to form, and says: "Neither pray I for these alone, but for them also which shall believe on Me through their word." Have you believed on Him through their word? Then you have His plain and positive assurance that He was praying for you then, that verse by verse you may take that prayer of prayers and say, "Jesus prayed this for *me.*" And now that He is the centre of the praises of heaven, whence no other echo floats down to us, what is our one permitted glimpse of the continual attitude and occupation of this same Jesus? "Who is even at the right hand of God, who also maketh intercession for us." That is what He is doing for you *now.*

Praying for His children
In that blessèd place,

Calling them to glory,
Sending them His grace;
His bright home preparing,
Faithful ones, for you;
Jesus ever liveth,
Ever loveth too.

12.

Take all Thy vessels, O glorious Finer,
Purge all the dross, that each chalice may be
Pure in Thy pattern, completer, diviner,
Filled with Thy glory & shining for Thee.
Prov. 25. 4.
Caswell Road.
Nov. 23. 1878.

What Thou wilt.

Do what Thou wilt! Yes, only do
What seemeth good to Thee:
Thou art so loving, wise, & true,
It must be best for me.

Send what Thou wilt, or beating shower,
Soft dew, or brilliant sun;
Alike in still or stormy hour,
My Lord, Thy will be done.

Teach what Thou wilt; and make me learn
Each lesson full & sweet,
And deeper things of God discern
While sitting at Thy feet.

13.

Say what Thou wilt; and let each word
  My quick obedience win;
Let loyalty & love be stirred
  To deeper glow within.

Give what Thou wilt; for then I know
  I shall be rich indeed;
My King rejoices to bestow
  Supply for every need.

Take what Thou wilt; beloved Lord,
  For I have all in Thee;
My own exceeding great reward
  Thou, Thou Thyself wilt be.

                                        Nov. 29.

The Lord hath done it. H. W.

Sing, O heavens! The Lord hath done it!
  Sound it forth o'er land & sea!
Jesus says, "I have redeemed thee,
  Now return, return to Me!"
O return, for His own life blood
  Paid the ransom, made us free
      Evermore & evermore.

This fair copy autograph was found in F.R.H.'s Manuscript Book Nº IX. See page 191.

MARCHING ORDERS

————

[*These "Marching Orders" were written by request, for the "Church Missionary Gleaner." The slight variations were made by F. R. H., when she copied and sent them to the Editor of the Woman's Foreign Missionary Society, in Philadelphia, March, 1879.—M. V. G. H.*]

"TELL IT OUT AMONG THE HEATHEN."

(Psalm 96:10, P.B.V.[1])

[1] P.B.V.: Prayer Book Version, the Book of Common Prayer.

King of Peace; Tell it out with ju - bi - la - tion though the waves may roar, That He

D.S.

sit - teth on the wa - ter - floods, our King for ev - er - more. Tell it

Tell it out among the nations that the Saviour reigns!
        Tell it out, tell it out!
Tell it out among the heathen, bid them burst their chains!
        Tell it out, tell it out!
Tell it out among the weeping ones that Jesus lives;
Tell it out among the weary ones what rest He gives;
Tell it out among the sinners that He came to save;
Tell it out among the dying that He triumphed o'er the grave.
        Tell it out, etc.

Tell it out among the heathen Jesus reigns above!
        Tell it out, tell it out!
Tell it out among the nations that His name is Love!
        Tell it out, tell it out!
Tell it out among the highways, and the lanes at home;
Let it ring across the mountains and the ocean foam;
Like the sound of many waters let our glad shout be,
Till it echo and re-echo from the islands of the sea!
        Tell it out, etc.

Frances Ridley Havergal, 1872.

MARCHING ORDER NO. I.

"Go ye therefore, and teach all nations."—MATTHEW 28:19.

"Go" does not mean "send." "Go" does not mean "pray." "Go" means "*Go!*" simply and literally.

Suppose the disciples had been content to take this command as most of us take it! Suppose three or four of them had formed a committee; and the rest had said, "You see if you cannot find a few suitable men to train and send to Rome, and Libya, and Parthia; and we will see what we can do about collecting funds, and anyhow subscribing a penny a week or a pound a year ourselves!" How would the good tidings of great joy and the glorious news of the resurrection have spread at that rate? But they did not subscribe—they went! Happily they had not silver and gold to give, so they gave themselves to their Lord and to His great work. Jesus had said, "I have given them Thy word"; and very soon "great was the company (margin, *army)* of those that published it," and grand were the results.

The company of those that publish the word of our God is very small in proportion to the numbers that are perishing for lack of knowledge. We are so accustomed to hear of the millions of India and China, or of the immense distances of America, that we get hardened to them. We do not take it in, that one man is standing alone among perhaps a hundred thousand dying souls; or placed alone in a district of a thousand square miles with forest and rapid, and days of travelling, between every station in that district. Even from one of the best provided centres of missionary work in India a friend writes that every missionary she has seen, whether clerical, lay, or lady worker, has work enough of his or her own to divide *immediately* among at least six more, if they would only come. Yet our Lord's very last command was "Go!"

The company is still smaller in proportion to those who might go if they only had the heart to go. Setting aside those who have not sought or found Christ for themselves, and who do not care to hear or read about these things, and those to whom the Lord has definitely closed this door by unmistakable circumstantial guidance, there must be, as a mere matter of figures, thousands of young Christians who might go or put themselves in training for going. Yes, *thousands,* who have "freely received" salvation for themselves, but are not ready to "freely give" themselves to their Saviour's own great work; not ready even to take the matter into consideration; not ready even to *think* of turning aside out of their chosen profession or comfortable home course. Yet the command, the last that ever fell from His gracious lips before He went up from the scene of His sufferings for us, still rings on, and it is "*Go!*" And He said, "If ye love Me, keep My commandments."

MARCHING ORDER NO. II.

"Go *ye*, therefore."—MATTHEW 28:19.

WHEN we read any general promise, faith appropriates it by saying "This is for *me!*" And then it becomes effectual; one receives it as surely as if it had been spoken to and for one's self alone. When we heard the word of the Lord Jesus saying, "Come unto Me, all *ye!*" we who believe on Him did not and do not hesitate to say, "That means me!" and to act upon the gracious invitation. Now, is it fair to accept His "*Come* ye," and refuse His "*Go* ye"? Is the first, with its untold blessings, to be appropriated personally, notwithstanding its plural form, and the second to be merely read as an interesting general command to whomsoever it may concern, but certainly not to ourselves?

As we have the unspeakable privilege and comfort of knowing that "all God's promises are for all God's children," so that you and I may claim every one unless we can show cause that it *cannot* apply to our case, so it must be that all God's commands are for all God's children, unless we can show cause that any one *cannot* apply to our case. Therefore it follows that, as the Lord Jesus Christ said "Go ye," the obligation lies upon each of His true followers to consider definitely, at least once in his or her life, whether the circumstances in which He has placed them do or do not definitely preclude them from literally obeying this distinct and most literal commandment.

If they are really thus precluded, the loving and loyal heart will be eager to find ways of obeying the spirit of it. But if *not* thus precluded, what then? To Him, your own Master, you must give account why you do not go! To Him you must "make excuse." To Him who gave Himself for you, and who knows exactly how much it is in your heart to "keep back" from Him. To Him who knows your secret preference for some other profession, or your reluctance to be tied to an absorbing life work; and who knows how you satisfy your conscience with offering Him the chips and shavings of your time and strength, a few odds and ends of work in the evenings or on Sundays, or a proportion of your time subtracted from "social claims," when you *might*, nobly, bravely, loyally, leave all and follow Him, responding to the Master's "Go ye," with "Here am I, send *me!*"

Have you thought of it in this light? If not, do not risk being among His disobedient servants, but take the matter direct to Himself, and say, "Lord, what wilt Thou have *me* to do? Make Thy way straight before my face!"

MARCHING ORDER NO. III.

"And Jesus came and spake unto them, saying, All power is given unto Me in heaven and in earth. Go ye therefore."—MATTHEW, 28:18, 19.

THE Father is the source of all power. For "Thine, O Jehovah, is the greatness and the power." The Holy Spirit is the Communicator of power, so that those who bring their emptiness to be filled with the Spirit may say: "Truly, I am full of power by the Spirit of the Lord." But our Lord Jesus Christ is the Depositary of the power. As in Him are hid all the treasures of wisdom and knowledge, so in Him is "the hiding of His power" who has delivered all things unto the Son of His love.

All power is given unto Him, our Saviour, our Master, absolutely, unlimitedly, eternally! It is such a happy thought. As love and knowledge gradually supplanted fear, how delighted, one might almost say how proud, the disciples must have been, as miracle after miracle revealed the power of Jesus of Nazareth. Yet they did not know that He had *all* power. *We* know it, for He has told us. Do not our hearts respond, "Worthy is the Lamb that was slain, to receive power!" "Let us be glad and rejoice, and give honour to Him!"

All power is given unto Him. First, power to give eternal life to as many as His Father has given Him; then power on earth to forgive sins; then power to uphold all things. And these really include all power in heaven and in earth. *All* power. For there is no other power at all. "There is no power but of God." All else that seems power is but the impotent weakness, the unavailing spite, of a vanquished foe. How quietly He disposes of it when He says, not to veteran apostles, but to His mere recruits: "Behold, I give unto you power … over all the power of the enemy!" What must the reserve be when this small delegated share is to overmatch "*all* the power of the enemy!"

All power is given unto *Him*. Not to us, for we could neither receive it nor use it. But to Him for us. For "all things are for your sakes." Joined to Him by faith we change our weakness into strength, for His power flows into us, and rests upon us. It is not that our weakness is made a little stronger, but that His strength is made perfect in our weakness. The power of the Head energizes the feeblest member.

But our Master makes no barren statements of unresultful positions. "All power is given unto Me." What then? "Go ye *therefore*." Who will take Him at His word, and, relying upon Jesus as our great Depositary of power, say, "*I will go in the strength of the Lord*"?

MARCHING ORDER NO. IV.

"Freely ye have received, freely give."—MATTHEW 10:8.

THE context shows that we must not content ourselves with applying this only to silver and gold. Those to whom the command was spoken neither possessed nor provided any. Far greater gifts had they received, far greater gifts were they to give.

What have we freely received? Our Bibles give us a threefold answer. 1. Love: God our Father says, "I will love them freely." 2. Justification: for we are "justified freely by His grace," and "by His blood." 3. Life: for He says, "I will give unto him that is athirst of the fountain of the water of life freely." And unto us has been preached this "gospel of God freely."

We are responsible not only for having received such gifts, but for knowing that *we* have received them, for "*we* have received ... the Spirit which is of God, that we might know the things that are freely given to us of God." The whole Bible is one long inventory of the things that are freely given to us, and yet we cannot reckon our wealth, for "*all* things are yours." Possessing the one unspeakable gift, Jesus Christ Himself, is "possessing all things."

"As every man hath received the gift, even so minister the same." How will you do this? Can you make it a question of shillings or pounds, dollars or cents? Is *that* what you have received? Is that *as* you have received? Will you not say, "I will freely sacrifice unto Thee"? Sacrifice! what? "I beseech you therefore, brethren, by the mercies of God, that ye present your bodies a living sacrifice." Is there not one reader of the *Church Missionary Gleaner* and of *Woman's Work*, who, having "received Christ Jesus the Lord," will go at His word, and "freely" make known the good news of life from the dead, and healing and cleansing through Him? There are so many who would delight to go, but whose way God has entirely hedged up. Are there none whose way is not so hedged up? He who spared not His own Son, but with Him freely gives us all things, is saying, very clearly and loudly, "Whom shall I send, and who will go for us?" Will any one who *might* say, "Here am I, send me!" refuse to say it?

MARCHING ORDER NO. V.

" *Therefore*, said He unto them, The harvest truly is great, but the labourers are few: pray ye *therefore* the Lord of the harvest that He would send forth labourers into His harvest."—LUKE 10:2.

LOOK at these two "therefores." The first gives the reason for one of our Master's sayings; the second for one of His commands.

I. The Lord Jesus sent out the seventy: not to go where they liked; not to take their chance of lighting on the right place or persons. Not to begin His work where it might or might not be followed up. But He sent them before His face into every city and place *whither He Himself would come.* Unto Him should the gathering of the people be, and the coming presence of the Lord of the harvest proved that a harvest was waiting for the reapers. "*Therefore* said He unto them, The harvest truly is great, but the labourers are few." Is it not encouraging to think that He, in whose ways is continuance (Isaiah 64:5), works in the same way now, and sends us, whether at home or abroad, into the places whither He, Himself, is coming? Whether an English or American Sunday school, or an Indian city, if the Master Himself sends His servant or His handmaid into it, it is because He, Himself, will come thither, blessing His reapers and receiving His sheaves. What an honour to be one of the "few" forerunners of the King, the herald of a silent yet real and mighty advent of the Very God of Very God!

II. Because the harvest is great and the labourers few, the Lord Jesus said, "Pray ye *therefore* the Lord of the harvest that He would send forth labourers into His harvest." If the fact remains the command remains. And the fact does indeed remain. And we have no excuse in not knowing it. We, the readers of the *Church Missionary Gleaner* and of *Woman's Work*, know how great the harvest is, and we know how few the labourers are. We cannot say, "Behold, we knew it not." The need is recognised, and the Lord has put the supply within reach of the voice of prayer and the hand of faith. He has told us what to do, and so now the responsibility rests upon us.

Perhaps we read these pages and we sorrow a little for the burden of the King of princes, and wish the accounts were more glowing. But we do not turn the passing emotion into obedient and faithful and purposeful prayer, and so our sluggard soul desireth and hath nothing. "*He* shall not fail nor be discouraged";

but if we fail as His "helpers" in this easiest and most graciously appointed share of His glorious work, how shall we hope to share in our Master's harvest joy, and what claim shall we have to join in the great harvest Hallelujah?

MARCHING ORDER NO. VI.

"Pray ye therefore the Lord of the harvest, that He would send forth labourers into His harvest."—LUKE 10:2.

MOST likely we never went to a missionary meeting in our lives but what we were told to pray for the work. We are quite used to it; we take it as a matter of course, and as the right and proper thing to be said. Nobody disputes for an instant that it is a Christian duty. But—*are we doing it?*

As it is an acknowledged obligation upon all who profess to love the Lord Jesus Christ that they should obey His commandments, it is clearly a real obligation upon us, upon you and me, to obey *this* commandment. And if we are not doing it, we are equally clearly directly disobeying our dear Master, and failing in the one test of personal love to Himself which He gave us in the same night in which He was betrayed.

Yes, *are we doing it?* Did you pray this morning what He bade you pray? Did you yesterday? Or last week? Surely it is no light thing to go on from day to day leaving undone a thing which we ought to have done, and about which His own lips gave the most explicit direction!

How often we have sorrowfully felt that "we know not what we should pray for as we ought!" Now here is something that we *know* we are to pray for. We know that it is according to His will, or He would not have bidden us ask it. And "if we ask anything according to His will, He heareth us." And if we know that He hears us in whatsoever we ask, we know that we have the petitions that we desired of Him. See what a splendid conclusion we reach! Oh, "pray ye therefore!" And if we thus pray, like little children, exactly what Jesus bids us pray, see if we do not find a real and probably conscious and immediate blessing in the very act—the floodgates opened, the spirit of grace and of supplication poured out, and the parched tongue filled with prayer and praise!

It is an immense help to be systematic in prayer. Many are finding it useful to take one of the seven petitions of the Lord's Prayer as the keynote of their own each morning. This brings "Thy kingdom come" to Monday morning. What if all the readers of the *Church Missionary Gleaner* and of *Woman's Work* should accept this as a continual reminder, and at least that *once* in each week join in fervent pleading of this Christ-taught petition, including in it the special one that the Lord would send forth labourers! Let us agree as touching this that we shall ask, in the obedience of faith and in the name of Jesus.

MARCHING ORDER NO. VII.

"Prayer also shall be made for Him continually."—PSALM 72:15.

VERY reverently, yet rejoicingly, let us accept these words exactly as they are written. Most likely we have read them with private revision of our own, and supposed them only to mean, "Prayer also shall be made *unto* Him continually." But see! there it is, "*For* Him"!

To many it may be a new thought, to some a very startling one, that we are not only to pray to our King, but *for* our King. Yet words cannot be plainer, and we lose untold sweetness by gratuitously altering them.

For whom shall prayer be made? There can be no doubt as to this. The glowing, far-reaching statements and promises of this most Messianic psalm could never apply to any mortal monarch. Solomon in all his glory is but the transparent typical veil through which we discern the far excelling glory of Messiah and "the glorious majesty of His kingdom." And the only word which for a moment seems to dim the clearness is this one, "*For* Him." But gaze once more, and let Love arise and come to the aid of Faith, and her quick eye shall pierce the shadow and trace new splendour through it. The more fervently we love any one, the more we want to pray for them. The very thought of the loved one is changed into prayer when it glows under the pressure of spirit.

Intercession is the very safety valve of love. We all know or have known this. There is solace and relief and delight in doing something for the object of our love; but the more our circumstances or ability or relative position hamper us and make us feel that our acts can bear but small proportion to our love (especially when gratitude is a large element in it), the more we feel that prayer is the truer and greater outlet. And when we have to feel that we really can *do* nothing at all in return for some remarkable kindness and affection, how exceedingly glad we are that we may and can *pray!*

Should there not be analogy here with the "depth and height" of the love of Christ? We have talked unhesitatingly, sometimes even a little boldly, of "working for Jesus." And even a glimpse of His "kindness and love" has been enough to set us working "for Him," as we call it. Then comes a clearer and brighter view of the "exceeding great love of our Master," and we are pressed in spirit, and all the work we ever could or can do for Him is seen to be just nothing, and oh how we *do* want to do more "for Jesus"! Now has not our God provided a beautiful safety valve for the full hearts of His loving children in this most condescending permission and command? Not only "to Him shall be given of the gold of Sheba," but "*prayer also* shall be made *for Him*"! Yes, we may pour out our hearts in prayer for Our King, besides spending our lives in working for Him. And I do not know that there is any purer and intenser joy than such prayer, pressed out by adoring love. There is no room for looking at self and difficulties and troubles and fears, when there is a gush of prayer summed up in "Father, glorify Thy Son!" We know that He hears this, and that we have the petitions that we desire of Him. And we go on, pleading His own great promises to the Son of His love, and rejoicing at the same time in their certainty; praying that Jesus may see of the travail of His soul and be satisfied, even in our own poor sinful hearts and lives, and in those for whom or over whom we are watching, and in myriads more; asking that the heathen may be given Him for His inheritance, and that all nations may call Him the Blessed One; and widening out to the grand prayer for Him with which the psalm closes, "And let the whole earth be filled with His glory! Amen, and amen." For this psalm is not only Messianic, but emphatically missionary, and so the prayer which is so graciously suggested and ordered in it is really the sum and culmination of all missionary intercession. And it is the spirit of it which ennobles and ought quite to transfigure all our missionary intercession. Let us keep the bright thought before us, that this is really, even if indirectly and unconsciously, making prayer "for Him"; and I would humbly say that if we take it up and so frame our petitions that they shall be directly and consciously "*for Him*," we shall hardly fail to find freshness of power and gladness in thus entering simply and literally this singularly bright vista of prayer which God has opened for us.

MARCHING ORDER NO. VIII.

"Talk ye of all His wondrous works."—PSALM 105:2.

I WONDER how many of us have observed this among our marching orders! And how many of us have been obeying it? Think of the last month, for instance, with its thirty days; on how many of those days did we talk of all His wondrous works? And if we did so at all, how much less did we talk about them than about other things!

Just consider what a power in the world *talking* is! Words dropped, caught up, repeated, then ventilated, combined, developed, set brains and pens to work; these again set the tongues to work; the talking spreads, becomes general, public opinion is formed and inflamed, and the results are engraven in the world's history. This is what talking can do when exercised about the affairs of "the kingdoms of the world and the glory of them." And we, who have been translated into the kingdom of God's dear Son,—we have tongues too, and what have we been talking about? How have we used this same far-spreading power? Only suppose that for every time each English-speaking Christian had talked about the day's news of the kingdoms of this world, he had spent the same breath in telling the last news of the kingdom of Jesus Christ to his friends and casual acquaintances! Why, how it would have outrun all the reports and magazines, and saved the expense of deputations, and set people wondering and inquiring, and stopped the prate of ignorant reviewers who "never heard of any converts in India," and gagged the mouths of the adversaries with hard facts, and removed missionary results and successes from the list of "things not generally known!"

God intends and commands us to do this. We often quote "All Thy works shall praise Thee, O Lord, and Thy saints shall bless Thee." That sounds tolerably easy; but what next? "They shall speak of the glory of Thy kingdom, and talk of Thy power." Is this among the things that we ought to have done and have left undone? Are we not verily guilty as to this command? "Lord, have mercy upon us, and incline our hearts to keep *this* law!"

Perhaps we say we have kept it; we have had sweet converse with dear Christian friends about the Lord's kingdom and doings, and surely that is enough? No! Read further; there is not even a full stop after "talk of Thy power." It goes on to say why, and to whom: "To make known to the sons of men His mighty acts, and the glorious majesty of His kingdom." Not just talking it over among our like-minded friends, exchanging a little information maybe; but talking *with purpose,* talking so as to make known what great things our God is doing, not gently alluding, but *making* the sons of men *know* things that they did not know were being done. Some very intelligent and well educated "sons of men" do not seem to know that there is such a thing as "His kingdom" at all; and whose fault is that? They do not and will not read about it, but they could not help the "true report" of it reaching their ears if every one of us simply obeyed orders and *talked,* right and left, "of the glory of Thy kingdom," instead of using our tongues to tell what we have just seen in the newspapers.

But the bottom of not talking is generally the not having much to talk about. When our Lord said, "Out of the abundance of the heart the mouth speaketh," He knew what was in man better than we know ourselves. We don't give ourselves the trouble to fill our hearts so that they cannot help overflowing. If we gave even the same time to supplying our minds with the telling, yes and thrilling facts, happening day by day in His kingdom, that we give to the "other things" reported in papers and periodicals, we should quite naturally talk of all His wondrous works. We should *want* to tell people what we had read and heard, not stale news picked up accidentally months ago, but something interesting from its very freshness in our own minds. When we have just read of a remarkable political event, or military victory, don't we forthwith *talk* about it? And if the next person we meet has not heard of it, do we hesitate to tell him all we know about it on the spot? It does not look as if we cared very much about our glorious Captain when we are not sufficiently interested in His latest victories in the mission field even to talk about them, *especially* to those who know nothing at all about them.

Now! what can we find, even in this month's magazine, which we can tell and talk about to those who have not read it? Begin at once!

MARCHING ORDER NO. IX.

"The Captain of their salvation."—Hebrews 2:10.

Who gives the marching orders? Ah! that is the secret of their force, that is the secret of the thrill with which they have reached the hearts of men and women who have hazarded their lives to carry them out, faithful unto death, in their noble, literal obedience. For it was the voice of the Captain of their salvation that they recognised and followed, as the "Go ye therefore" fell upon their opened ears.

Of *their* salvation only? Is He not also the Captain of *our* salvation? Has not the Father given Him to be a Leader and Commander, and exalted Him to be a Prince and a Saviour for *us*? And shall His marching orders be disregarded, whatever they are, by one whose salvation He brought with His own arm, whose life He bought with His own blood?

For think how His Divine captaincy was won! No lightly or easily assumed leadership was that. A solemn and mysterious qualification of unknown sorrows and agonies was necessary. "For it became Him, for whom are all things, and by whom are all things, in bringing many sons unto glory, to make the Captain of their salvation perfect through sufferings." Through wounding for our transgressions, through bruising for our iniquities, through chastisement and stripes, "through death," yes, "the *suffering* of death," did our Lord Jesus Christ pass to be made our perfect Captain, so that no soldier of His should ever have to endure any hardness or any fight of afflictions, without that real personal sympathy from his Master which can only be the outflow of real, personal experience of the same. Oh, think of "the things that He suffered," over and above the great atoning suffering on the cross, just that He might personally know our little sorrows, and personally enter into our insignificant sufferings, and succour us in them with His own mighty help! "For in that He Himself hath suffered, being tempted, He is able to succour them that are tempted." Think of all that detail of suffering through His lonely life and lonelier death being just the detail of *love*,—love freshly marvellous in this aspect.

And now that the suffering is over, and the Captaincy is won, and we are enrolled to be His faithful soldiers and servants unto our lives' end, is it to be merely a nominal thing on our side? It was no nominal thing on His side. The sufferings of the Lord Jesus were not nominal, and His exaltation to be a Prince as well as a Saviour is not nominal; then shall we dare to treat His orders as merely nominal, and as something to be comfortably explained away, according to circumstances? Oh, if our loyalty were as literal as His love, if our obedience were as literal as His sufferings, would there, could there be such want of volunteers to go where He has plainly set up His standard, and such want of free-handed pouring into His treasury, and such want of brave speaking out of heart-abundance, and such want of fervent, faithful, persevering echoes of the great prayer, "Father, glorify Thy Son!"

But if, by His grace, we are seeking honestly to obey His marching orders, we shall find that the very effort of obedience will quicken our faith and love; the more we listen the more real and familiar will the voice of our Captain become, and the closer we follow the clearer will be our realization of His Leadership. And then we shall take up the exultant words: "Behold, God Himself is with us, for our Captain!" and know the full blessedness of being ranged under the victorious banner of Immanuel.

> Fierce may be the conflict,
> Strong may be the foe,
> But the King's own army
> None can overthrow.
> Round His standard ranging,
> Victory is secure,
> For His truth unchanging
> Makes the triumph sure.

Response. Joyfully enlisting
   By Thy grace Divine,
  We are on the Lord's side;
   Saviour, we are Thine.

Chosen to be soldiers
 In an alien land;
" Chosen, called, and faithful,"
 For our Captain's band;
In the service royal,
 Let us not grow cold;
Let us be right loyal,
 Noble, true, and bold.
Response. Master, Thou wilt keep us,
   By Thy grace Divine,
  Always on the Lord's side,
   Saviour, always Thine!

"Say amongst the heathen, that the Lord reigneth."—Psalm 96:10.

Succoth. 87, 87, 77.

1 Heralds of the Lord of glory!
      Lift your voices, lift them high:
   Tell the gospel's wondrous story,
      Tell it fully, faithfully;
   Tell the heathen midst their woe
   Jesus reigns, above, below.

2 Haste the day, the bright, the glorious!
      When the sad and sin-bound slave
   High shall laud, in pealing chorus,
      Him who reigns, and reigns to save.
   Tempter, tremble! Idols, fall!
   Jesus reigns, the Lord of all!

3 Christians! send to joyless regions
      Heralds of the gladdening word;
   Let them, voiced like trumpet legions,
      Preach the kingdom of the Lord;
   Tell the heathen, Jesus died!
   Reigns He now, though crucified.

4 Saviour, let Thy quickening Spirit
      Touch each herald lip with fire;
   Nations then shall own Thy merit,
      Hearts shall glow with Thy desire:
   Earth in jubilee shall sing,
   Jesus reigns, the eternal King!

Rev. William Henry Havergal, 1827.

(No. 881, "Songs of Grace and Glory.")

OUTLINES OF ADDRESSES.

Original manuscript in F.R.H.'s handwriting. This was found in her Manuscript Book Nº VIII, one of her "Verses on Texts." See pages 559–568 of Volume I of the Havergal edition.

THE seven following subjects are copied from F.R.H.'s outlines of the addresses given in her parlour, November and December, 1878. The illustrations which enriched them, the sacred songs or solos aptly introduced, the stirring appeals, the beseeching voice, passed unrecorded. But they are not forgotten; hence the testimony of her village hearers: "Miss Frances *still* speaks to us; her voice follows us, especially the words, 'Be ye holy, for I am holy'; and 'without holiness no man shall see the Lord.' She was God's mouth to us."

EXTRACTS FROM LETTERS TOUCHING
THESE MEETINGS.

To S. G. Prout.

Nov. 6th, 1878. ... "Now I want you to do me a good turn. I want you to find a minute to spare, when you are bringing other needs before your Master, to ask for me a real great blessing on an open Bible class which I am starting this evening. I don't know who will come, few or many, but I want real converting grace poured out, and I want to be enabled so to speak of Jesus that they may be won to Him. There is the centre. How it just goes through one, when one touches upon His own beloved name! And how we do want Him to be understood and loved!"

To J. K.

Nov. 7th. ... "I don't know how to thank you enough for your prayers. I made a delightful start last night with about thirty. I think there is a fair prospect next time of filling every available space and chair. I started at once on the *Christian Progress* lines (giving each the explanatory paper, and requesting all to read the chapters every day). The very first result showed I was justified, for that same evening our dear little Christian maid got leave (indeed I think they asked her) to read the evening portion in the kitchen. Mr. and Mrs. Tucker and many others seem taken with the idea of joining me and the other fifteen thousand readers. I can't think why other workers don't see the value of this Union, as I do. What *can* you do better for those whom you have won, or are trying to win, than thus to ensure them two good meals a day! I am most thankful that I was distinctly led to start at once with the *C.P.* Union.

"F. R. H."

LEPROSY. (*Nov. 6th,* 1878.)

LEVITICUS 13.

Symptoms. Various outwardly. But always:
    (1) Deeper than the skin (ver. 3; Isaiah 1:5, 6).
    (2) Spreading (ver. 7). Compare white hair (Hosea 7:9.)
    (3) Infectious.
Effects of leprosy:
    (1) Isolation (ver. 45).
    (2) Exclusion from the camp (ver. 46; Revelation 21:27).
    (3) No cure but by the direct hand of God (Numbers 12:10, 13).
    (4) Progressing unto death. ("Grew worse," Mark 5:26; 2 Timothy 3:13; Matthew 12:45.)

1. Not some, but all, have sin (Romans 3:23).

2. Feeling makes no difference; sin is *a fact* (Psalm 51:5).

3. In leprosy the priest first looked (Psalm 119:132; Hebrews 4:13; John 2:25), then pronounced the leper unclean (John 5:22).

4. Priests could neither cure nor cleanse; Jesus does both. Compare Hosea 5:13 and 6:1. Compare Matthew 8:3, Exodus 15:26.

5. *How* Jesus heals. "He was wounded for our transgressions, He was bruised for our iniquities; the chastisement of our peace was upon Him, and with His stripes we are healed" (Isaiah 53:5).

A devoted minister going to dwell in the leper island of Molokai, voluntarily leaving his home and his country, exposing himself to contagion, disease, and death, out of love to the souls of the poor outcast lepers dwelling there, is the nearest illustration. Still he could not take the leprosy *instead* of the lepers. But the Lord Jesus was "made sin for us, who knew no sin, that we might be made the righteousness of God in Him" (2 Corinthians 5:21). Took sin *upon* Him, *off* us.

6. Only one case in which the leper was pronounced clean (Leviticus 13:12, 13), if *all* covered. So "only acknowledge" (1 John 1:9; Isaiah 64:6; Romans 7:18), and turned white (Isaiah 1:18; Psalm 51:7).

7. Christ always healed leprosy without *delay* or *means* (Matthew 8:3. Contrast Matthew 15:23 and John 9:7). "The Same" now, immediate cleansing in His blood.

8. Nothing to hinder except not coming. "Ye will not come to Me, that ye might have life" (John 5:40.)

9. Claim this by faith. Healing *only* in God's way (Acts 3:16, 4:12, 14:9). Say, "Heal me, O Lord, and I shall be healed" (Jeremiah 17:14).

10. Then praise! "And one of them, when he saw that he was healed, turned back, and with a loud voice glorified God" (Luke 17:15). "O Lord my God, I cried unto Thee, and Thou hast healed me" (Psalm 30:2, 103:2, 3).

11. *Continual* healing and *continual* cleansing. "The blood of Jesus Christ His Son cleans*eth* us from all sin" (1 John 1:7).

HOLINESS, AND BEING GOD'S OWN. (*Nov. 13th*, 1878.)

"And ye shall be holy unto Me: for I have severed you from other people, that ye should be Mine."—LEVITICUS 20:26.

I. WHAT God would have us be—holy unto Himself. *First step* to holiness is seeing our sinfulness (Leviticus 13:12, 13; Isaiah 6:5).

1. *Need* of holiness. "Holiness, without which no man shall see the Lord" (Hebrews 12:14, 21, 27).

2. *Command.* "Be ye holy, for I am the Lord your God" (Leviticus 20:7). "But as He which hath called you is holy, so be ye holy in all manner of conversation; because it is written, Be ye holy for I am holy" (1 Peter 1:15, 16).

3. *Enabling grace* in Himself. "I am the Lord which sanctify you" (Leviticus 21:8). Sevenfold (Philippians 2:12, 13).

4. *Promise and purpose.* "For whom He did foreknow He also did predestinate to be conformed to the image of His Son" (Romans 8:29). "For this is the will of God, even your sanctification" (1 Thessalonians 4:3). "Whom the Lord doth choose, he shall be holy" (Numbers 16:7).

II. Three reasons for holiness.

1. Because He is holy. "Who is like Thee, glorious in holiness?" (Exodus 15:11.) "Holy, holy, holy, is the Lord of hosts" (Isaiah 6:3). Effect on Isaiah, ver. 5.

God the Father holy: "Holy Father" (John 17:11). God the Son: "Thine Holy One" (Acts 2:27). God the Spirit: "the Spirit of holiness" (Romans 1:4). Trinity: "Holy, holy, holy, Lord God Almighty, which was, and is, and is to come" (Revelation 4:8).

Holiness is the dividing line between saints and sinners (Psalm 97:10–12; Revelation 15:4).

Wonderful that this *holy* God loves us and wants us to be holy, and will make us "partakers of His holiness" (Hebrews 12:10).

2. Because God has separated His people unto Himself. Israel a type of believer's separation (1 Corinthians 10:11, τύποι).

(1) Command. "Wherefore come out from among them, and be ye separate, saith the Lord" (2 Corinthians 6:17).

(2) Promise. "And I will receive you, and will be a father unto you, and ye shall be My sons and daughters, saith the Lord Almighty" (2 Corinthians 6:17, 18). "Seemeth it but a small thing unto you, that the God of Israel hath separated you from the congregation of Israel, to bring you near unto Himself?" (Numbers 16:9.) "But know that the Lord hath set apart him that is godly for Himself" (Psalm 4:3). Illustration: The brave, the loyal, the soldiers of unswerving allegiance and obedience, are chosen for the royal body guard, "The Queen's Own!"

3. Because He wants us to be His *own*. *"Mine."*

(*a*) To be His people (Hebrews 8:10). I am your God (Leviticus 20:8).

(*b*) Servants (John 20:10; Psalm 116:16). Master (John 13:13).

(*c*) Children (Jeremiah 3:4). Father (Jeremiah 3:19).

(*d*) Bride (Hosea 3:3). Husband (Hosea 2:19, 20; Isaiah 54:5).

(*e*) Peculiar treasure (Psalm 135:4). Exceeding great reward (Genesis 15:1).

(1) To His "own." Don't only say, "*We* are Thine" (Isaiah 63:19), but "*I* am Thine" (Psalm 119:94). He replies: "Fear not, for I have redeemed thee, I have called thee by thy name; thou art Mine (Isaiah 43:1). *"For"* price indeed (1 Corinthians 6:19, 20; 1 Peter 1:18, 19; 2 Samuel 7:21–24). Evidence given (Malachi 3:16, 17). Have you not a word for Jesus? (Malachi 1:6.)

(2) But *are* you His own? Illustration: Forlornness of a child not belonging to anybody. Do you "belong to Christ"? If not, you belong to a secret owner whose slave you are (Romans 6:16). But

"Come to be Thine, yea Thine alone."

(Of the touching tenderness of F. R. H's appeal no record can be given.)

CHRIST OUR LAW-FULFILLER. (*Nov. 20th*, 1878.)

"These are the commandments which the Lord commanded Moses for the children of Israel in Mount Sinai."—LEVITICUS 27:34.

These commands, what we have read in Exodus and Leviticus. Two great divisions, the ceremonial law and the moral law. Christ the *end* of both (Romans 10:4).

I. Ceremonial law. Burdensome and costly. Contrast, "My yoke is easy and My burden is light" (Matthew 11:30).

All performed through priests. "And every priest standeth daily, ministering and offering oftentimes the same sacrifices, which can never take away sins: but this Man, after He had offered one sacrifice for sins for ever, sat down on the right hand of God. For by one offering He hath perfected for ever them that are sanctified" (Hebrews 10:11, 12, 14).

All this only "a shadow of good things to come"; "a shadow of heavenly things" (Hebrews 10:1, 8:5). Describe the shadow, and contrast it with the substance. Christ the substance. *He* is a continual object lesson, teaching of Himself and His offices and of our need of atonement. Hebrews 9:9, 10: "until." Christ the end of all this.

II. Moral law. This law was

1. *Reflection of God's holiness*; forbidding all contrary, enjoining all accordant. Witness to the law is placed within us—conscience, *answering* only if awake. Illustration: If a witness is drugged he can give no evidence, no response. Sin drugs the conscience (Romans 7:11–16).

2. *The moral law is summed up in two great commandments* (Matthew 22:37–40). These are put in one word by St. Paul, love! "Love is the fulfilling of the law" (Romans 13:10).

3. The moral law is *not done away with.* "Verily I say unto you, Till heaven and earth pass, one jot or one tittle shall in no wise pass from the law till all be fulfilled" (Matthew 5:18). Some confuse between the ceremonial and the moral law. Christ not only did *not* destroy the moral law, but gave it a fuller meaning and a wider reach, applying all to the heart as well as our outward observance (Matthew 5:21–45). "Sin is the transgression of the law" (1 John 3:4). "The soul that sinneth it shall die" (Ezekiel 18:4). The Commandments are read in our Communion Service, and the prayer after each is, "Lord, have mercy upon us, and incline our hearts to keep this law." It would be well if this was done in chapels also.

4. If the moral law is not done away with, it *has got to be fulfilled.* Mark the word: not *one* thing done that ought not to be, not one left undone. *Not* doing harm is *not* fulfilling the law; you will never get to heaven by what you have *not* done. It would be no excuse for a servant who had broken a china vase to say,

"I have not broken the window *and* the china." "For whosoever shall keep the whole law, and yet offend in *one* point, is guilty of all" (James 2:10). This is not my saying but God's; and Christ says, "The word that I have spoken, the same shall judge him in the last day" (John 12:48). Illustration: If only *one* link was broken in the chain let down to pull you out of the shaft of a mine, the danger is the same, even if every other link were unbroken.

Tests: "Search the Scriptures" (John 5:39); and, "Thou shalt love the Lord thy God with all thy heart, and with all thy soul, and with all thy mind" (Matthew 22:37). Even if all else kept, have you *searched* the Scriptures, have you loved God with all your heart?

Therefore, "all have sinned and come short of the glory of God" (Romans 3:23). Illustration: Describe the ice crevasses in the pass of St. Theodule; travellers roped to the guide; if that rope breaks once only, danger. Besides, God says, "Neither shall they cover themselves with their works" (Isaiah 59:6).

5. Christ is the end of *this* law *for* righteousness *to* every one that believeth.

The very first thing He said He came to do. "Think not that I am come to destroy the law or the prophets: I am not come to destroy, but to fulfil" (Matthew 5:17). God said, "He will magnify the law and make it honourable" (Isaiah 42:21). Christ said: "Lo, I come: in the volume of the book it is written of Me. I delight to do Thy will, O My God: yea, Thy law is within My heart" (Psalm 40:7, 8). *Why* did Jesus Christ live thirty-three years? *Why* not simply come down to die? It was to do for us just what we have not done and could not do, "fulfil all righteousness." This had got to be done by some one for us; that is, instead of us. "For as by one man's disobedience many were made sinners, so by the obedience of one shall many be made righteous" (Romans 5:19). "Many be made righteous," but *who* are they? All them that believe, "for the righteousness of God which is by faith of Jesus Christ is unto all and upon all them that believe" (Romans 3:22). So Jesus is our "righteousness" (1 Corinthians 1:30). "And this is His name whereby He shall be called, THE LORD OUR RIGHTEOUSNESS" (Jeremiah 23:6). Then we may say, "All our righteousnesses are as filthy rags" (Isaiah 64:6); and, "I will greatly rejoice in the Lord, my soul shall be joyful in my God, for He hath clothed me with the garments of salvation, He hath covered me with the robe of righteousness" (Isaiah 61:10).

6. *Therefore* let us keep the commandments. *Jesus* said, "If ye love Me, keep My commandments" (John 14:15). "For the love of Christ constraineth us" (2 Corinthians 5:14). Love evidenced by obedience, "He that hath My commandments, and keepeth them, he it is that loveth Me" (John 14:21); and faith evidenced by works, "Even so, faith if it hath not works is dead" (James 2:17).

What about seeking for *all* the commandments of the Lord? This is a further step; He wants us to "seek for *all* the commandments of the Lord your God (1 Chronicles 28:8). He wants us to keep "*all* ... always." "Oh that there were such an heart in them, that they would fear Me, and keep *all* My commandments always" (Deuteronomy 5:29). Because, "the Lord commanded us to do all these statutes, to fear the Lord our God for our good always" (Deuteronomy 6:24). And God promises in the new covenant, "I will put My laws into their mind, and will write them in their hearts" (Hebrews 8:10). Pray, "Make me to go in the path of Thy commandments" (Psalm 119:35); and "Write all these Thy laws in our hearts, we beseech Thee." It is very humbling when the Holy Spirit's light flashes upon some command of our God which we have never observed, and of course have never kept. Do ask that blessed Spirit to show you not only your sin in not keeping His commands, but also the remedy, the precious blood of Christ. Come to that Fountain, and you will find the cleansing, sanctifying, and overcoming power of the blood of the Lamb.

In conclusion, what are *you* going to do about: 1st, believing; and 2nd, obeying? John 14:21, 23: "He that hath My commandments and keepeth them, he it is that loveth Me." "If a man love Me, he will keep My words." "Moreover by them is Thy servant warned, and in keeping of them there is great reward" (Psalm 19:11).

———————

THE VOICE FROM THE MERCY SEAT. (*Nov. 27th*, 1878.)

"And when Moses was gone into the tabernacle of the congregation to speak with Him, then he heard the voice of One speaking unto him from off the mercy seat that was upon the ark of testimony, from between the two cherubims: and He spake unto him."—NUMBERS 7:89.

WHAT has this to do with us? Everything—for God "hath in these last days spoken unto us by His Son" (Hebrews 1:2).

I. The Ark.   II. The Mercy Seat.   III. The Voice from it.

I. The Ark. See Exodus 25:10–16. "When we find Christ in the law, that law becomes gospel."

A.—1. The ark was of shittim wood and gold, typifying the human and Divine nature of the Lord Jesus.

2. "Overlaid with gold," not two parts separable, but all the wood overlaid with gold; hence Christ was "perfect God and perfect man."

3. Crown of gold round about the mercy seat; type of "royalty," and the "throne of grace."

4. Rings and staves for carrying the ark; the gospel to be preached to all nations.

5. In the holy of holies it was dark; contrast in heaven, the holiest of all, no created light needed.

B.—1. What was the ark for? To contain the tables of God's law. Refer to our last lesson; Christ our law-fulfiller: "Thy law is within my heart" (Psalm 40:8).

2. The ark was described and ordered and provided (1) *before the law was written* (Exodus 31:18, and 32:15, 16); so Christ was foretold and provided before; never a moment when Christ was not: (2) *before the law was broken*, God foresaw; so before He gave the law which He knew would be broken He provided a Mediator and Substitute to keep it perfectly.

3. The ark contained the *second* set of tables; first broken, never pieced together again (Exodus 32:19), renewed set (Exodus 34:1, 4, 28). Adam broke the Divine law, therefore the first covenant at an end. So have we broken the law, therefore no covenant of works avails. If one party breaks conditions, a contract is null. Therefore God renewed and placed it in better hands; put it into an ark which held it safe till all it required was fully accomplished.

II. The mercy seat.

1. Gold only. Mercy God's prerogative (Mark 2:7).

2. Exact size. "And thou shalt make a mercy seat of pure gold; two cubits and a half shall be the length thereof, and a cubit and a half the breadth thereof" (Exodus 25:17). As *wide* as Christ's whole nature; *no wider*, because no mercy *out* of Christ. See Hebrews 10:28, 29, and 2 Corinthians 5:19.

3. Kept in place by the crown. Sovereignty and kingly righteousness. "A God all mercy were a God unjust:"

4. The mercy seat covered the tables of the law. "God shut up its curses and hushed its thunders." Now, it is not the law that speaks condemnation, but the blood of Jesus speaks acquittal from the mercy seat.

> "Thine was the sentence and the condemnation,
> Mine the acquittal and the full salvation."

5. The mercy seat, place of God's especial presence and glory and meeting place (Psalm 80:1; Exodus 25:22). "There will I meet with thee," in *Christ.* Promise and fulfilment.

III. The voice from the mercy seat.

1. It was when Moses went to the appointed place that he heard the voice. We shall not hear God's voice of mercy unless we come to Christ. "Jesus said unto him, I am the Way, the Truth, and the Life, no man cometh unto the Father but by Me" (John 14:6). "Wherefore He is able also to save them to the uttermost that come unto God by Him" (Hebrews 7:25).

2. Moses heard it from the mercy seat. Contrast Genesis 3:8; Psalm 85:8; Acts 10:36.

3. Voice speaking "unto *him*"; so it is individual.

4. Spoke for direction and guidance.

Application. What do we know of God speaking to us from the mercy seat? He speaks through Jesus. "Jesus speaks and speaks to thee," etc. He says, "I have somewhat to say unto thee" (Luke 7:40), and "I have yet many things to say unto you" (John 16:12). Are we saying, "Master, say on," and "Speak, Lord, for Thy servant heareth"? And Jesus said, "The words which I speak unto you, they are spirit and they are life" (John 6:63). Don't we want these "words"? and reply, "I will watch to see what He will say unto me" (Habakkuk 2:1). Illustration: the Queen's dinner party. Surely every voice would be hushed to hear her speak. Do we ever listen for the "still small voice"? He says, "I will speak comfortably unto her" (Hosea 2:14; Isaiah 50:4). Let our response be, "I will hear what God the Lord will speak" (Psalm 85:8), and "Say unto my soul, I am thy salvation" (Psalm 35:3).

He appoints the meeting place, all the day long He is stretching forth His hands to us. He *is* speaking, are we neglecting to hear His voice? "How shall we escape if we neglect so great salvation, which at the first began to be spoken by the Lord?" (Hebrews 2:3). "He that rejecteth Me and receiveth not My words hath One that judgeth him: the word that I have spoken, the same shall judge him in the last day" (John 12:48, 49).

He still "waits." "Come *now* and let us reason together, saith the Lord, though your sins be as scarlet they shall be as white as snow; though they be red like crimson they shall be as wool" (Isaiah 1:18).

Think *who* it is that waits. Jesus the Son of God. "For we have not an high priest which cannot be touched with the feeling of our infirmities, but was in all points tempted like as we are, yet without sin. Let us *therefore* come boldly unto the throne of grace, that we may obtain mercy, and find grace to help in time of need" (Hebrews 4:15, 16). "Having therefore, brethren, boldness to enter into the holiest by the blood of Jesus, by a new and living way which He hath consecrated for us through the veil, that is to say, His flesh; and having an High Priest over the house of God; let us draw near with a true heart and in full assurance of faith" (Hebrews 10:19–22).

FORGIVENESS. (*Dec. 4th*, 1878.)

"Pardon, I beseech Thee, the iniquity of this people according unto the greatness of Thy mercy, and as Thou hast forgiven this people from Egypt, even until now."— NUMBERS 14:19.

NEWS of forgiveness is only interesting to those who are conscious of sin.

I. Who pleaded. II. Who forgave. III. Who was forgiven. IV. Extent of forgiveness.

I. Who pleaded: Moses.

(1) *Mediator.* "Moses His chosen stood before Him in the breach to turn away His wrath, lest He should destroy them" (Psalm 106:23). So Christ: "For there is one God and one Mediator between God and men, the man Christ Jesus" (1 Timothy 2:5).

(2) *Intercessor.* Had not shared the sin. So Christ, "who needeth not daily, as those high priests, to offer up sacrifice, first for his own sins and then for the people" (Hebrews 7:27). "It is Christ that died, yea, rather that is risen again, who is even at the right hand of God, who also maketh intercession for us" (Romans 8:34). Moses never pleaded in vain except for himself. "And the Lord said, I have pardoned according to thy word" (Numbers 14:20). So Christ, "and I knew that Thou hearest Me always" (John 11:42).

II. Who forgave? *Thou.* "Forgiving iniquity and transgression and sin" (Exodus 34:7). "Who can forgive sins but God only?" (Mark 2:7.)

III. Who was forgiven? "This people," described as "a disobedient and gainsaying people" (Romans 10:21). "A stubborn and rebellious generation, a generation that set not their heart aright, and whose spirit was not steadfast with their God." "How oft did they provoke Him in the wilderness and grieve Him in the desert" (Psalm 78:8, 40).

IV. Extent of forgiveness. "From Egypt," all along, murmurings, rebellings, idolatry, stupidity, etc., "until now." Climax of their sin, "were it not better for us to return into Egypt?" "Let us make a captain and let us return into Egypt."

"All the congregation bade stone them with stones" (Num. 14: 3, 4, 10). Yet, "Thou *hast* forgiven this people"; "and the Lord said, I have pardoned according to thy word." (Then turning to the piano, F. R. H. sang "Loving all along."[1])

> TRAMP, tramp on the downward way,
> With seldom a stop and never a stay,
> Loving the darkness, hating light,
> Our faces set towards eternal night!
> Each has answered God's cry,
> "Why will ye die? turn ye! turn ye!"
> "Not I, not I!"
> We have bartered away His gems and gold
> For the empty husks and the shadows cold;
> We have laugh'd at the Devil's tightening chains,
> And bidden him forge them strong!
>   And God has kept on loving us,
>   Loving all along.
>
> The love still flows as we tramp on;
> A sorrowful fall in its pleading tone;
> "Thou wilt tire in the dreary ways of sin;
> I left My Home to bring thee in!
> In its golden street stand no weary feet,
> Its rest is glorious, its songs are sweet!"
>   And we shout back angrily, hurrying on
>   To a terrible home, where rest is none:
> "We want not your city's gilded street,
> Nor to hear its constant song!"
>   And still God keeps on loving us,
>   Loving all along.
>
> And the tender Voice pursues each one:
> "My Child, what more could thy God have done?
> Thy sin hid the light of heaven from Me,
> When alone in the darkness I died for thee!
> Thy sin of this day, In its shadow lay,
> Between My face and One turned away!"

---

[1] "Loving all Along." Words by S. G. Prout (from "Never say Die"). Music by F. R. H. Published by Hutchings & Romer.

And we stop and turn for a moment's space,
Flinging back the love in the Saviour's face,
To give His heart yet another grief, and glory in the wrong!
    And Christ is always loving us,
      Loving all along.

One is bending low before the King,
And the angels listen with quivering wing;
He *has* entered the City and sings its hymn,
While the gold of its street through tears is dim!
"To Him who so loved me and washed me white,
To Him be all honour and power and might!"
That marvellous love no sin could move,
Waited, and wearied not, sought and strove!
To us, through the darkness, the Voice still calls
From the gleaming heights of the jasper walls;
To the long kept places our welcome waits,
    Amid the exultant throng.
  Chorus.—And God will still be loving us,
      Loving all along,
    And God will still be loving us,
     .Loving all along!

Apply all this to our own case. Why do we need forgiveness? Conscience tells, *if* enlightened. Sins of deed, word, thought, commission, omission, sins of this day, can you recollect? yesterday? all the year? since childhood? (Psalm 25:7.) We forget, but God records *all*, every one either forgiven or unforgiven. Not *one* who is unforgiven enters heaven; "and there shall in no wise enter into it anything that defileth, neither whatsoever worketh abomination or maketh a lie" (Revelation 21:27).

Then take the first and great command, "Thou shalt love the Lord thy God with all thy heart and with all thy soul and with all thy mind"; are we not "guilty"? Then see Psalm 78:22. "They believed not in God, and trusted not in His salvation." Believed not! trusted not! Guilty under *all* these counts, and none the less for not seeing we are; sin itself blinds us. Let each say now, "Father I have sinned." What then? "There is forgiveness with Thee, that Thou mayest be feared" (Psalm 130:4, 7). "To the Lord our God belong mercies and forgivenesses, though we have rebelled against Thee" (Daniel 9:9). That's much, but we want more. Then, "Thou Lord art good and ready to forgive" (Psalm 86:5). God is "*ready*," but perhaps we are hardly "ready," and say, "I don't feel my sins enough" (you don't find that in the Bible); but God meets us with the promise that He will give us "*repentance* and *remission*" (Acts 5:31).

Perhaps it is the opposite with some of you, and you are saying, "My sins are too great to be forgiven." Then "Let the wicked forsake his way, and the unrighteous man his thoughts; and let him return unto the Lord, and He will have mercy upon him; and to our God, for He will abundantly pardon" (Isaiah 55:7, and 1:18; Psalm 103:3).

How can this be? "Through this Man is preached unto you the forgiveness of sins" (Acts 13:38).

How so? "If we confess our sins, He is faithful and just to forgive us our sins" (1 John 1:9). *Faithful* because He promised; *just* because Christ bore the punishment, purchased the forgiveness. Talk about "free" forgiveness; free to us, but cost Him blood. So, "God for Christ's sake hath forgiven you" (Ephesians 4:32; 1 John 2:12). What is bought *is* bought. So *in* Him "we have redemption through His blood, the forgiveness of sins" (Ephesians 1:7; Psalm 85:2).

Will you believe the message to-night? "I have blotted out, as a thick cloud, thy transgressions, and as a cloud thy sins: return unto Me; for I have redeemed thee" (Isaiah 44:22), (Illustration: There was once a deaf mute, named John. Though he never heard any other voice, he heard the voice of Jesus, knew it, loved it, and followed it. One day he told the lady who had taught him, partly on his fingers and partly by signs, that he had had a wonderful dream. God had shown him a great black book, and all his sins written in it, so many, so black! And God had shown him hell, all open and fiery, waiting for him because of all these sins. But Jesus Christ had come and put His *red hand,* red with the blood of His cross, all over the page, and the *dear* red hand had blotted all John's sins out; and when God held up the book to the light He could not see one left! (Isaiah 43:25.)

Don't fear to take forgiveness at once. God does not want long processes— He looks into the heart. If while sitting here any want to turn from sin and be forgiven, that is repenting; if any are saying, "Yes, I know it is all true of me," that is confession; and "If we confess our sins, He is faithful and just to forgive us our sins." Now take forgiveness, for "you, being dead in your sins and the uncircumcision of your flesh, hath He quickened together with Him, having forgiven you all trespasses" (Colossians 2:13). "When Jesus saw their faith, He said unto the sick of the palsy, Son, thy sins be forgiven thee" (Mark 2:5). This same Jesus is here to-night.

What else? Shall sins come up again? In the new covenant God declares, "I will be merciful to their unrighteousness, and their sins and their iniquities will I remember no more" (Hebrews 8:12). Then Micah 7:18, 19.

1. *Pardoneth.* (Illustration: "Ah, Willie," said a strong man in tears, "it's forgiven sin breaks a man's heart," etc.)

2. Will subdue.

3. Will cast all their sins into the depths of the sea,

"Blessed is he whose transgression is forgiven, whose sin is covered" (Psalm 32:1).

THE BRAZEN SERPENT. (*Dec.* 11*th*, 1878.)

"And the Lord said unto Moses, Make thee a fiery serpent, and set it upon a pole: and it shall come to pass, that every one that is bitten, when he looketh upon it, shall live. And Moses made a serpent of brass, and put it upon a pole, and it came to pass, that if a serpent had bitten any man, when he beheld the serpent of brass, he lived."—Numbers 21:8, 9.

No mistake about the application of the type, Christ Himself gives it: "And as Moses lifted up the serpent in the wilderness, even so must the Son of Man be lifted up: that whosoever believeth in Him should not perish, but have eternal life" (John 3:14, 15).

I. What the sin was.
1. Discouragement (Psalm 106:24; 78:22).
2. Spake against God and against Moses.
3. Untruth: "no bread ... no water."
4. Dissatisfaction with God's provision of manna.
All this was "tempting Christ" (1 Corinthians 10:9).

II. The punishment. "And the Lord sent fiery serpents among the people, and they bit the people; and much people of Israel died" (ver. 6). The bite fatal, so the Devil's bite of sin. Implied in the Hebrew word, "flying serpent" (Isaiah 30:6). Satan "goeth about," nothing out of his reach but what is in Christ's hand. "Fiery," beginning of the worm that never dies, the "everlasting burnings." Probably the bite induced fever and thirst.

III. The remedy. The serpent of brass, same form but no venom. "Christ made sin for us, who knew no sin" (2 Corinthians 5:21). The *curse* (Genesis 3:14; and Galatians 3:13). Thus *doubly* Christ was made a curse for us.

"*Lifted up.*" So on Calvary, conspicuous, known, seen. So now: "And I, if I be lifted up from the earth, will draw all men unto Me" (John 12:32); every time Christ is proclaimed.

"*Must be* lifted up" (ver. 14); compare Christ's "*musts*" for our sakes.

Remedy devised by God. "Yet doth He devise means" (2 Samuel 14:14); contrary to human reason or supposition.

No other remedy. Suppose an Israelite thinking the remedy too simple, too unlikely, trying some "first rate stuff," or going to the priest or physicians; all in vain, only *one* appointed way (Acts 4:12).

All could see, so no excuse; all may look now.

Result of looking: life. "It shall come to pass"; "It came to pass."

Instant cure. "When he looketh"—that moment—*now!*

Are you looking now? If so, "*saved.*" If not, *unsaved*; the deadly bite working certain death. Suppose an Israelite saying, "Yes, all very true; but I'm tired to-night," or "going to have my supper." If you found the serpent had bit you, you would soon drop forks. (*e.g.*: Describe a real scene at a supper table where many were assembling after a mission service. There were some still unsaved ones there, and the sting of sin was so bitter that they could not eat, could not conceal their distress; and then and there we all knelt down, and then and there they looked and lived. Then, with every face bright, cured, and happy, how joyful that supper time was.)

Must look for yourself, no one *can* look for you. "Whom I shall see for myself, and mine eyes shall behold, and not another" (Job 19:27). In the last day no choice about looking then, but too late for the saving look.

Command: "Look unto Me, and be ye saved, all the ends of the earth: for I am God, and there is none else" (Isaiah 45:22). No option; going on in disobedience as well as danger, if you don't look.

Waiting till better: device of Satan.

No condition. "Whosoever," only *look*, "every one," "any man." "And this is the will of Him that sent Me, that every one which seeth the Son, and believeth on Him, may have everlasting life: and I will raise him up at the last day" (John 6:40).

Must know you are bitten, or you won't look. Fancy an Israelite saying, "Don't see that I'm so very poorly; not *quite* right perhaps, but not like *that* poor fellow dying there," etc., etc.

Cure never failed. Ver. 9: "*Any* man … he *lived.*" "If *any* man … shall live for ever. … He that believeth on Me hath everlasting life" (John 6:51, 47). Believe it! Israelite didn't need to feel his pulse, he *lived* and *knew* it. Take God at His word, and He will take you at yours.

Not only *not perish,* but *live, have* everlasting life. What does that imply? Everlasting salvation, joy, light, love, and with Him (1 Thessalonians 5:10). "Father, I will that they also whom Thou hast given Me be with Me where I am, that they may behold My glory" (John 17:24). Contrast the word *perish* and life. God knows what that word "perish" means. Jesus knows, and therefore *pleads* with you. The Devil knows, and hushes up the meaning. You don't know yet, but it's a terrible certainty.

What will it be to be lost for want of a look! Devil taunting through all eternity. "You *might have been* saved if you would have looked, and you wouldn't." And you risk *this* if you don't look to-night.

You who have looked:

1. *Tell others*; fancy an Israelite cured, and quietly watching others dying, without a word.

2. *Keep on looking.* "Looking unto Jesus, the author and finisher of our faith" (Hebrews 12:2). Many a little *snap* after the great bite is cured, but looking is both prevention *and* cure. "But mine eyes are unto Thee, O God" (Psalm 141:8). "Unto Thee lift I up mine eyes" (Psalm 121:1).

3. The "*look*" now, the long blessed gaze then. "Thine eyes shall see the King in His beauty" (Isaiah 33:17).

> "Is it for me to see Thee
> In all Thy glorious grace,
> And gaze with endless rapture
> On Thy belovèd face?"

THE CONTINUAL BURNT OFFERING. (*Dec. 18th,* 1878.)

"And thou shalt say unto them, This is the offering made by fire which ye shall offer unto the Lord; two lambs of the first year without spot day by day, for a continual burnt offering. The one lamb shalt thou offer in the morning, and the other lamb shalt thou offer at even. And a tenth part of an ephah of flour for a meat offering, mingled with the fourth part of an hin of beaten oil. It is a continual burnt offering, which was ordained in Mount Sinai for a sweet savour, a sacrifice made by fire unto the Lord."—NUMBERS 28:3–6.

EACH of the offerings had a *special* teaching.

I. The circumstances of this offering, typifying Christ.

1. *God calls it "My* offering"; compare "God will provide Himself a lamb" (Genesis 22:8).

2. *Two lambs.* (1) Clean. (2) Valuable. (3) Good for food. (4) Harmless. (5) Meek. (6) Isaiah 53:6, 7; "*we* like sheep," therefore Christ the *Lamb*.

3. *Without spot* (1 Peter 1:18, 19; 2 Corinthians 5:21; 1 John 3:5).

4. *Offering* made by fire. All circumstances of the *burnt* offering indicated suffering and wrath (Leviticus 1:5–9). Killed, blood shed, flayed, cut into pieces, all burnt. So Christ suffered for sins (1 Peter 3:18), "died for" (1 Corinthians 15:3), "gave Himself for" (Galatians 1:4). *Real* (Luke 22:44; Isaiah 58:5; Psalm 22:14–17, 32:8[1]). "By Thine agony and bloody sweat, by Thy cross and passion"; took *all that.*

Why was fire needful in these sin offerings? Shows the wrath descending on the victim instead of the offerer. (Describe lightning conductor; the flash, once descending on that, passes into the earth, spent, never returns, never strikes again.)

5. *Offered at the door of the tabernacle* (Exodus 29:42). The Israelite could not go in to worship, could not reach the shewbread and the candlestick, nor even approach the veil, without passing by the altar of burnt offering.

So Christ's offering of Himself for us, His atonement, is the *very beginning*. All past and present worship, without it, is mockery and iniquity, prayers and hymns and all.

6. *Day by day.* This the special point of the type, teaching that continual sin needed always atonement. The sin goes on day by day (if you get a glimpse of that you would not dare to lie down to-night without an interest in the atonement); but *now* the sin offering is done away. Why? because the Messiah was cut off but not for Himself. "*He shall cause the sacrifice and the oblation to cease*" (Daniel 9:27). The shadow passed when the substance came. Christ made it to cease when He died (Hebrews 10:1, 11, 12).

One sacrifice for sins *for ever*. Done, finished. "I have finished the work which Thou gavest Me to do" (John 17:4). "It is finished" (John 19:30). "Christ was *once* offered to bear the sins of many" (Hebrews 9:28). An Israelite could never come and *not* find the altar there.

Morning and evening sacrifice, possibly, showed atonement for age and youth.

7. *It was a sweet savour.* Would God let His Son suffer *in vain?* Fire goes out when the fuel is burnt; no more flame. Justice satisfied, God satisfied (Ephe-

[1] Psalm 32:8 is very likely a mistake (either F.R.H.'s or the Nisbet typesetter's): F.R.H. likely meant another Scripture reference.

sians 5:2). "Christ also hath loved us, and hath given Himself for us, an offering and a sacrifice to God of a sweet smelling savour," does not mean that God was pleased to see Jesus suffer, but the result of those sufferings (John 10:17). If God is *satisfied*, why not *you*?

II. What will you do about it?

1. Are you unconverted or anxious? See the Israelite laying his hand on the head of the sin offering, showing the transfer—accepting it as substitute. ("This is my act and deed.") When you own the sin, and own Christ's death as your substitute, then "*it shall be accepted for him*"—the sacrifice burnt up instead of the offerer. Nothing to do, nothing else will do. Security is not your *feeling* satisfied, but God's *being* satisfied. (Isaiah 42:21.) Then now "behold," etc. (John 1:29.) He still says, "Behold Me, behold Me" (Isaiah 65:1).

2. You who have accepted the offering *are* accepted in the Beloved. What *must* follow? "Who His own self bare our sins in His own body on the tree, that we, being dead to sins, should live unto righteousness; by whose stripes ye were healed" (1 Peter 2:24). "Forasmuch then as Christ hath suffered for us in the flesh, arm yourselves likewise with the same mind: for he that hath suffered in the flesh hath ceased from sin, that he no longer should live the rest of his time in the flesh to the lusts of men, but to the will of God" (1 Peter 4:1, 2). "And that He died for all, that they which live should not henceforth live unto themselves, but unto Him which died for them, and rose again" (2 Corinthians 5:15). Titus 2:14: "That He might redeem us from all iniquity," not only from wrath. See Hebrews 10:10: "Once for all," that you might be *sanctified*.

As the continual burnt offering showed always the present atonement for sins that are past, so it shows the continual cleansing for the present. "The blood of Jesus Christ His Son cleans*eth* us from all sin" (1 John 1:7). Must not, dare not, continue in sin, etc. "What shall we say then? ... How shall we, that are dead to sin, live any longer therein?" (Romans 6:1, 2.)

III. *Christ, as the Lamb, is an eternal type.* See Revelation 6:16: "the wrath of the Lamb." Will it fall on us? No wrath of the Lamb, for those washed in the blood of the Lamb. "There is therefore now no condemnation to them which are in Christ Jesus, who walk not after the flesh but after the Spirit" (Romans 8:1). We shall for ever have to do with the Lamb of God. "Worthy is the Lamb that was slain to receive power, and riches, and wisdom, and strength, and honour, and glory, and blessing. And every creature which is in heaven, and on the earth, and under the earth, and such as are in the sea, and all that are in them, heard I saying, Blessing, and honour, and glory, and power, be unto Him that sitteth upon the throne, and unto the Lamb for ever and ever" (Revelation 5:12, 13; 7:9, 14, 17).

SONG OF SOLOMON 1:1–8.

Ver. 1: "The song of songs, which is Solomon's."

Solomon a type of Christ. This "song of songs" is Christ's song, the song which He puts into the hearts and lips of His children. Contrast with the "vanity of vanities" in Ecclesiastes. This song is also a type of the "new song." Christ's children are His bride, even if ever so weak and unworthy.

Ver. 2: "Let Him kiss me with the kisses of His mouth."

Kiss the token of love. "Mouth"; this gives a clue to the meaning of "grace is poured into thy lips" (Psalm 45:2); and "the gracious words which proceeded out of His mouth" (Luke 4:22). Applied to our own hearts He says, "I will speak comfortably (margin) to her heart" (Hosea 2:14). Have we experience of this, His words coming sweetly to our hearts? If so, we have had the "kisses of His mouth." If not, "oh taste and see"; "incline your ear"; "watch to see what he will say" (Habakkuk 2:1); and then say, "Master, say on."

"For Thy love is better than wine" (ver. 2) "Wine" is the symbol of all *earthly* refreshment and joy. Jesus gives the new wine of His love, and says, "Drink, yea, drink abundantly, O beloved" (Song of Solomon 5:1); "Yea, come, buy wine and milk" (Isaiah 55:1).

Ver. 3: "Because of the savour of Thy good ointments Thy name is as ointment poured forth."

Let us begin with the second clause, "Thy name." How sweet the name which is above every name, Jesus (Philippians 2:9). "Ointment": "the house was filled with the odour of the ointment" (John 12:3). Oriental odours surpassingly fragrant. Appeal to you who really love the Lord Jesus; does not His very name bring a *thrill*, a fragrance? Jesus! If His name is *in* our hearts, its fragrance should fill the house. Sometimes this is not till the box is *broken*; many tongues not loosed till dying. But why thus? Why not, if we have the ointment, pour it out now, and be *living* witnesses, not waiting to be *dying* witnesses, for Him. Let others take knowledge of you that you have been with Jesus (Acts 4:13).

What is His name? "Wonderful, Counsellor, the mighty God, the everlasting Father, the Prince of Peace" (Isaiah 9:6).

"*Because of*"; because not merely ointments poured forth, but the unfailing supply within. O name of *infinite* sweetness! Ointments denote its manifold preciousness. Perhaps we first come to love Christ for what He has *done*, for the pouring forth of the ointment; but then we go on to love Him for what He is, to rejoice in the ever unfolding sweetnesses of His perfections (1 Peter 2:7).

"*Therefore* do the virgins love Thee." Because He is *what* He is, so full of infinite sweetness and beauty and love and grace (Zechariah 9:17). "Love Thee." Do *we?* How worthy Jesus is of our love, of our desire to love Him. If we can't yet say, "Lord, Thou knowest all things, Thou knowest that I love Thee" (John 21:17), can we say "the desire of our soul is to Thy name," and "to the remembrance of Thee" (Isaiah 26:8)? If so, be encouraged, for "He will fulfil the desire of them that fear Him" (Psalm 145:19). The promise is to them that *fear*, not even love.

Ver. 4: "Draw me, we will run after Thee: the King hath brought me into His chambers: we will be glad and rejoice in Thee, we will remember Thy love more than wine: the upright love Thee:"

"Draw me." The more we find our utter helplessness, the more we find His strength and sufficiency. His "drawing" always comes before our "coming"; our cry to Him only the echo of His still, small voice (John 6:44). It is a great mistake to think this great truth a reason for despair—it is reason for hope and confidence. If we have any desire, He gave it, and that is His *drawing.* Now—don't check and stifle His drawing; yield—run.

"Drawing" is the token of everlasting love (Jeremiah 31:3). We desire because He *draws*; He draws because He *loves*. But let us "run," "press," "strive." No sauntering (1 Corinthians 9:24). "We *will* run": resolution, will, energy. Perhaps we feel we have no will, no energy; see how we need *all* from Him. If we have it, He gave it; if we have it not, we can only get it from Himself. Sweet paradox, in such *running* there is *rest*.

"Draw *me, we* will run." We should not come alone, but when "drawn" seek to win others. "After Thee." The secret of true running the heavenly race after Jesus is following close in heart, keeping near, abiding in Him, and also following His steps (1 Peter 2:21). Our collect well expresses this, "daily endeavour ourselves to follow the blessed steps of His most holy life." It is not running after anything or any one else, but Jesus only—"after *Thee.*"

"The King hath brought me into His chambers." What is this? His dwelling place, His pavilion, the secret of His tabernacle, the secret of His presence (Psalm 90:1; 27:5; 31:20; 25:14). This is no dream, but a reality. There is a "secret of His presence," into which He brings His children. Not at first perhaps, but by degrees. "I have yet many things to say unto you, but ye cannot bear them now" (John 16:12).

We could not explain it to another, *what* it is to feel Jesus near, to feel that we *are* brought into His chambers, but it is real, and unutterably sweet. It is such shelter in trouble, and such added sweetness in joy. What treasures of happiness are ready for us if we will but come to Jesus! "We will rejoice," etc. We *shall* if he thus brings us (Psalm 45:15).

"We will remember." How often forget! Contrast Isaiah 49:15. Fulness of theme. We may remember part and yet forget the rest, love resolving and redeeming—living and dying. Let us *try* to remember and say Isaiah 26:8. Remember also *experience* of love—treasure it up for dark days. Communion Service: "To the end that we should always remember the exceeding great love of our Master and only Saviour, Jesus Christ"; and He meets us in remembrance (Isaiah 64:5).

"The upright love Thee." Illustrate. Would it be "upright" if one entered service, were living and receiving wages, etc., and yet *did* nothing? If we profess to serve Christ, it is not "upright" if we do nothing for Him. Secret of lack of love, we mourn over coldness, then up and *work* for Jesus.

Ver. 5: "Black, but comely." "Black" (Isaiah 64:6; Romans 3:23, 7:18). Can't see this but with opened eyes; the more light, the more we *see* the darkness. First we only mark sins of act, then word, thought, motive, feeling, then the whole array of uncountable omissions, the good we *might* have done and did not; then we resolve and try and fail, and find the utter sinfulness of which all this is only the fruit. If we saw it *all at once* we should be overwhelmed.

"But comely!" How? (Ezekiel 16:14.) "My comeliness which I had *put* upon thee."

Ephesians 5:26, 27: church composed of individuals. "Tents and curtains." Explain simile. "And let the beauty of the Lord our God be upon us" (Psalm 90:17). But how shall *we* have this beauty? "Even the righteousness of God," etc. (Romans 3:22.) Do you believe? Ask your own hearts now, "Dost thou believe on the Son of God?" Then it is upon you, even if never realized before; *you* are justified and clothed in His beauty. Do not think it matters not; you can stand in nothing else before God. (Matthew 22:11–13.)

Ver. 6: "Look not upon *me*," but "Behold, O God our shield, and look upon the face of Thine Anointed" (Psalm 84:9). God seeing us in Christ our representative. "The sun" throwing light upon it. Is it so with us? Backsliding, yielding under the hot sun of temptation or persecution? Then plead this verse.

"My *mother's* children were angry with me," *i.e.* earth's "children of this world" angry. This should not discourage, because our *Father* and His children will not be angry.

"Made me keeper," *e.g.* Sunday-school teachers; apply and appeal to them; only in cultivating our own vineyard are we likely to keep others'. But not only to keepers of other vineyards this applies; "mine own vineyard" applies to *all*, each has a vineyard which should bring forth fruit unto God. (Hosea 10:1.)

Ver. 7: "Tell me, O Thou whom my soul loveth, where Thou feedest, where Thou makest Thy flock to rest at noon: for why should I be as one that turneth aside by the flocks of Thy companions?" Our "tell me" always the echo of His whisper, "I have somewhat to say unto thee."

"O Thou whom my soul loveth" comes *after* "we will remember." Love of longing, not yet of nearness. Proof of love is the desire of nearness. There are three desires here: 1st, "tell me *where*"; 2nd, food (Matthew 5:6); 3rd, rest. At noon heat, weariness. Mark, not rest at night. Some one told me "we must look forward for rest," but no, rest *now* "at *noon*." With most of you it is now morning, but quickly morning rises into noon, and sooner or later you will crave *rest*. (Psalm 23:2.) (Job 34:29.) (Isaiah 26:3, 12.) (Matthew 11:28.) Only "Thou," no other can make. "Makest"—sometimes He makes us weary first (Job 16:7), that He may win us to rest.

"Why should I be," in the margin "is veiled." Idea here is threefold.

(1) The bride was veiled when in the presence of strangers, orientals only unveiling at home and in the presence of most intimate friends.

(2) Veil is the token of distance, restraint, separation; contrast this with Christian communion.

(3) Veil the token of dim vision, veils and dimness constantly go together. Contrast, when the veil shall be taken away (2 Corinthians 3:16–18). From the veiled to veilless vision.

"Flocks of thy companions." Wonderful title! See also John 15:15.

Ver. 8: Gentle rebuke implied, why do we not know? The Holy Spirit is promised to show all things, to teach all things, to guide into all truth.

"O Thou fairest." Compare chap. 2:10, 14, and 4:1, 8; Ephesians 5:27. "Go thy way forth by the footsteps of the flock."

Our church services are often undervalued, *they* are the footsteps of Christ's flock for centuries back. The Te Deum and Communion Service are glorious echoes of the church militant. Distinct blessing on Christian intercourse. (Malachi 3:16; Luke 24:14, 15.)

Memoirs often a help, tracing the footsteps of others.

One path trodden by *all* the flock, prayer; they "come boldly unto the throne of grace."

(Unfinished.)

EVERLASTING LOVE.

"I have loved you, saith the Lord."—MALACHI 1:2.

THIS is only the old old story: but it is written with the finger of God; graven with the diamond pen of His unchangeable truth on the rock of His everlasting purpose; traced in golden letters on records of the universe; printed in characters of living, shining, glowing light on hearts of believers; written by the Spirit of the living God, not with ink but blood, precious blood of Christ, blood shed on the cruel cross for us. Query, is it written on our hearts? If not, O blessed Saviour, write it now; write if it be but the first line of this glorious inscription on every heart *here* and *now*.

"I have loved you, saith the Lord. *Yet* ye say, Wherein hast Thou loved us?"

I. "*Herein.*" (1) "Herein is love, not that we loved God, but that He loved us, and sent His Son to be the propitiation for our sins" (1 John 4:10). Sovereign love. "The Lord did not set His love upon you, nor choose you, because ye were more in number than any people; for ye were the fewest of all people; but because the Lord loved you" (Deuteronomy 7:7, 8). "*Not* that we loved God." Our heart echoes this "not." "His thoughts are not our thoughts." The natural heart says, "God can't love me because I don't love Him."

(2) "In this was manifested the love of God toward us, because that God sent His only begotten Son into the world" (1 John 4:9). Gift of God (John 3:16). "Gave," unto death. Love of the Son answering. "Greater love hath no man than this, that a man lay down his life for his friends" (John 15:13).

(3) In quickening: "But God, who is rich in mercy, for His great love wherewith He loved us, even when we were dead in sins, hath quickened us together with Christ" (Ephesians 2:4, 5). Do we think enough of this further proof of His love; we who are not "dead in trespasses and sins," but feel and live?

(4) In adopting. "Behold," etc. (1 John 3:1.) Are any here feeling they have no part in this; outside the home and Father's love? say now, "I will arise and go to my Father" (Luke 15:18).

(5) Bearing and carrying (Isaiah 63:9). *Has* He not "borne"? *has* He not carried? Even if we can't feel (3) and (4), we must own *this*.

Query: "Wherein" has thus a fivefold answer. Turn from His book to the book of our own lives, and count up the proofs of this love. Include "chastening" (Hebrews 12:6).

II. *How?* Double answer (John 17:23, and John 15:9). "As" (subject for study).

Perfect love, εἰς τέλος, (John 13:1).

Sacrificing love. Father (Romans 8:32), Son (John 15:13); both combined in Romans 5:8.

Everlasting love (Jeremiah 31:3). This brings us to:

III. ~~*When*~~ He loved us. (1) Before the foundation of the world (compare John 17:23, 24, 26).

(2) When we were yet sinners (Romans 5:8; compare Hosea 3:1; Isaiah 48:8, 10). "I knew."

(3) Before we recognised it (1 John 4:19, Ezekiel 16:8). "When," "then," "time of love."

(4) After backsliding (Hosea 14:4).

(5) In death as in life (Song of Solomon 8:7). "Cannot quench," not those things in Romans 8:35, climaxing in violent death. For, Isaiah 43:2 and Deuteronomy 33:27.

(6) Through eternity: "Everlasting life Thou givest, Everlasting love to see." All included in that wonderful εἰς τέλος (John 13:1).

IV. Results of this love.

(1) Believing. Love begets love, this is the condition of the manifestation of love.

(2) Outward mark, "For the love of Christ constraineth us" (2 Corinthians 5:14, 15; John 14:21, 23; John 16:27).

(3) What if *resultless?* (Lamentations 1:12.) Appeal and application [no notes recorded].

V. Great question: how may we know that everlasting love is ours? (compare John 6:44 with Jeremiah 31:3).

How we yearn over the title, "disciple whom Jesus loved"! It applies to us also: "O man greatly beloved." May we all be able to say, "We have known and believed the love which God hath to us."

EVERLASTING LIFE.

"For the wages of sin is death; but the gift of God is eternal life, through Jesus Christ our Lord."—ROMANS 6:23.

THIS is the most important of all subjects, concerns each one: "that ye may know that ye have eternal life; and that ye may believe on the name of the Son of God" (1 John 5:13).

I. *What* is the gift? To value it, we must look at the contrast: eternal death. He hath "set the one over against the other."

The Holy Spirit has used only *one* word in the original for the duration of both (Matthew 25:46). No use imagining an alternative; no annihilation, etc., etc.; instinct as well as revelation tells this. After all arguments of infidels (overturned again and again by voices which they won't go to hear and books which they won't read) there remains an awful *if* which none can set aside. *If* they turn out to be wrong, if the Bible be true, *then* "what remaineth?" "blackness of darkness for ever," "where their worm dieth not, and the fire is not quenched" (Mark 9:46). But there is no real "if": God has revealed all this.

Now contrast: "gift of eternal life"; life which no decay can touch, no death can shadow; in which the grave will be only "parenthesis," not "period"; gift worthy of Giver. Why eternal? because not mere prolongation of *our* life, but Christ's own eternal life given *to* us, as His mortal life was given for us. "Because I live, ye shall live also" (John 14:19). (Colossians 3:3.) Can Christ, the Very Life, die? Faith makes one with Him, and partakers of His life (Luke 10:42).

Describe eternal life. 1st, negatively; no sin, sorrow, pain, death, etc.: 2nd, positively; life of perfect love, knowledge, holiness, bliss.

II. *Who* is the Giver? The Father, "the gift of God is eternal life" (Romans 6:23). The Son, "I give unto them eternal life" (John 10:28). The Holy Spirit, "the Spirit giveth life" (2 Corinthians 3:6). Gift of the triune Jehovah; "King eternal, immortal, invisible." Value of the gift enhanced by consideration of the Giver.

III. *Who* may have the gift? First, the thirsty ones (Isaiah 55:1; John 7:37). But even if not hitherto among these, and cannot claim "Blessed are they which do hunger and thirst after righteousness" (Matthew 5:6), a wider offer still. Secondly, *"whosoever* will" (Revelation 22:17): you and I.

IV. *Why* we may have eternal life. (1) Because God has promised it *for us to* Christ (Titus 1:2). "In hope of eternal life, which God, that cannot lie, promised before the world began." He holds the promise for us (illustration of promise made *to* parents *for* a child). (2) Because Jesus has taken our sin and its wages, *death*, upon Himself, in our stead.

V. *How* we may have eternal life. "Only believe." "Believe on the Lord Jesus Christ, and thou shalt be saved" (Acts 16:31). "Verily, verily, I say unto you, he that heareth My word, and believeth on Him that sent Me, hath everlasting life, and shall not come into condemnation; but is passed from death unto life" (John 5:24). What can hinder? only one thing; we can't receive a gift in a *full* hand: "Nothing in my hand I bring." It is offered on no other terms, can be had on *no* other, than as a "free gift." Gift too, not to friends but to *debtors* and *enemies* (Romans 5:6, 7, 8). How debtors? Take one point only (Mark 12:30): "Thou shalt love the Lord thy God with all thy heart, and with all thy soul, and with all thy mind, and with all thy strength; this is the first command," absolute debt: who can dare say we have rendered obedience to this one command. Verily "nothing to pay." What if we persist in clinging to false hopes and vain efforts! (Illustration. Five sailors were clinging to the broken mast of a sinking ship in Dublin Bay. A rope was thrown to them. At the trumpet signal "Now!" they were to loose their hold of the mast, and trust themselves to the rope. Four did so, and were hauled safe to shore. The fifth hesitated to let go, and was lost!)

VI. *When* we may have eternal life. This very day and hour. Now! "He that believeth on the Son hath everlasting life" (John 3:36). "Verily, verily, I say unto you, he that believeth on Me hath everlasting life" (John 6:47). No reason *in* delay: "If you tarry till you're better, you will never come at all." (Illustration. One summer's evening a traveller hired a boat on a wide and apparently safe river. He was warned not to go too far, not to *delay* in turning, at a signal of danger, where the current swept down the falls of Niagara. He knew there *was* danger; after amusing himself, still floating down the stream, he fell asleep. Onward, downward, went the boat, past the signal post; the sleeper slept on. Passers by on the shore shouted, "Stop!" "stop!" The sleeper woke; too late to turn back, one cry of despair—and he was hurled to the depths beneath.)

But perhaps you have eternal life without knowing it. Listen to God's word: (1 John 5:11). Rest your soul on this, and make God a liar no longer, but believe the record that "God hath given to us eternal life, and this life is in His Son."

NOTES FOR A YOUNG WOMEN'S CHRISTIAN ASSOCIATION MEETING.

I HAVE sometimes wondered at the knowledge of the Holy Spirit implied in Psalm 51. But we see every operation of the Holy Spirit mentioned before the time of David. In our February subject we saw the sevenfold operations of the Holy Spirit. For this month observe the grouping. But first glance at Psalm 143:10: "leading" being a specialty with Israelites in the desert. The Prayer Book version is beautiful: "Let Thy loving Spirit lead me forth"; compare Romans 15:30. We do not dwell enough on the *real* and *personal* love of the Spirit. He is no abstract idea, but a *loving Person*. His love is the fountain of His work and operations.

1. Renewing. 2. Comforting. 3. Sealing. 4. Grieving at our sins. 5. Helping our infirmities. 6. Shedding abroad the love of God. 7. Making intercession for us. All these flow from love, as sevenfold rays from pure white light.

First group: Judges 3:10, 6:34. In these verses notice, the power of the Spirit enabling His chosen instruments for work or warfare seems the leading idea. For our comfort in sense of weakness link with 1 Corinthians 12, "Same Spirit" seven times. Apply this to reading of or observing the work of the Spirit in others. Judges 6:34; 1 Chronicles 12:18; clothed in "glorious apparel" (Isaiah 63:1), denoting the gifts and graces of the Holy Spirit, clothing outwardly as well as filling inwardly. Connect with the prayer, "Endue them with innocency of life"; clothe, invest, array.

Second group: 1 Samuel 10:6, 10; 16:14. Temporary influences of the Spirit.

Third group: Psalm 51:11, 12; 139:7; 143:10. Group how you will, so comprehensive.

I. See three titles of the Spirit: 1. Holy, as He is in Himself. 2. Good or loving, as He is *towards* us. 3. Free, the essence of His work in us. 2 Corinthians 3:17: "glorious liberty."

II. (1) Deity and omnipresence. (2) Actual possession and possible loss. (3) Upholding. (4) Loving and leading.

Psalm 51:11: "Take not Thy Holy Spirit from me"; contrast with Haggai 2:5. Key to the difficulty. There may be (1) influence of the Spirit upon the mind, (2) *conscious* presence of the Spirit; and both these may be withdrawn. But the promised or the covenanted gift of the Spirit "remaineth." If we have taken hold of the "covenant," *all* covenanted blessings are ours, "everlasting" as the covenant itself (Luke 10:42). Solemn to think of the passing impulses of the Spirit, but joyful to know that His real work abideth.

The promise in Haggai 2:5 has a special Association connection (see context, ver. 4), "work," building of the spiritual temple; we are called to bring the stones, the precept and the promise for us. If we are *not* working, not obeying the precept, we lose our claim to the promise; how many promises are lost thus.

Fourth group: 1 Chronicles 28:19, compare ver. 12, Spirit and Jehovah; hence Deity of the Spirit.

In writing, whether for the press or letters, write for God, and He will teach ourselves by it. I would advise *written* preparation for Sunday school or Bible class teaching.

Fifth group: 2 Chronicles 15:1, 20:14, 24:20. Three instances typical of our work. 1. Azariah, calling to those who are "without God" to turn to Him, leading them to *prayer.* 2. Jahaziel, encouraging and strengthening those who *are* on the Lord's side, leading them to *praise.* 3. Zechariah, witnessing against sin and departure from God; compare Nehemiah 9:30.

What account have we to give of our Young Women's Christian Association membership under these three points!

NOTES OF F. R. H.'S ADDRESS TO Y.W.C.A. AT SWANSEA, THURSDAY, APRIL 17, 1879.

HOSEA 3:1–3. One of the most precious double promises of the Bible. Is it for us? See who it is for—if we answer to the description. The question need never be, are we *good* enough, but are we *bad* enough, for claiming the promise!

I. Our personal position.

1. Beloved, yet faithless. (Isaiah 43:7–10.) The love of the Lord (Malachi 1:2; 1 John 4:10; Jeremiah 31:3; John 13:1). "Yet" treacherous, and He knew it (Isaiah 48:8). "Who look to other gods" (Isaiah 26:13). Who "love flagons of wine," *i.e.* earthly joys, craving, etc. Guilty under the first command (Matthew 22:37). Does this describe us? Or do we remember His love "more than wine" (Song of Solomon 1:4)?

2. *"Bought"* (ver. 2). *"So* I bought her," because no other way would do. The faithless one must be made His own by right. (1 Corinthians 6:19, 20.) "Redeemed with the precious blood of Christ" (1 Peter 1:19). There is the force of the *"so,"* by Thine agony and bloody sweat, by Thy cross and passion (Isaiah 53:3); *so* He bought her.

Another view of "so" is just contrary to what we should have expected, "let him alone" (Hosea 4:17). "And I said after she had done all these things, Turn thou unto Me" (Jeremiah 3:7).

"Bought her *to Me*." Boaz purchased Ruth to be his wife (Ruth 4:8, 10); only money there, here blood. What intensity of desire is implied! How Jesus must have *wanted* us! "In His *love* and in His pity He redeemed."

II. The Lord's personal covenant with us.

1. "Thou shalt abide for Me." "Shalt" has a fourfold meaning: (1) *Purpose* (Psalm 4:3; 2 Timothy 4:18; Isaiah 43:21; Romans 11:4). Now: "seemeth it but a small thing unto you, that the God of Israel hath separated you from the congregation of Israel, to bring you near to Himself?" (Numbers 16:9.) (2) *Command*. "Shalt," "for," "in," "with me." (3) *Promise* (Psalm 90:1). Shall abide; compare "ye shall abide in Him" (1 John 2:27). Christ undertakes our part, because we *cannot* (Zechariah 9:7). And the new covenant was established (Hebrews 8:8–10). Won't you trust Him to do this (Isaiah 38:14)? (4) *Resolve* (Psalm 90:17, 18 [mistake, possibly she meant Psalm 89:17, 18], with Jude 24).

2. "Many days"; compare Matthew 28:20, *i.e.* "all the days," and Exodus 21:6.

3. "So will I also be for thee." In the past (Galatians 2:20), but see the *present*; *e.g.* a mother "lives for" her child, thinking, caring, watching, providing, managing, directing, *cherisheth*. "*So* will I also be for thee," in every detail; *e.g.* Romans 8:31, Psalm 56:9.

Who then is willing to enter this full, blessed, complete covenant? Personal, "*with me*" (2 Samuel 23:5; Ecclesiastes 3:14). *Now*, "come," etc. (Jeremiah 50:5.)

"If you are not *for* Him, you are *against*," (Luke 11:23,) your side against God, God's side "*against* thee" (Ezekiel 35:3). But take a contrasted glimpse; if you are willing to be "*for Him*," you have the King's own answer, now, "Behold, I am for you" (Ezekiel 36:9; Hosea 2:19, 20; Isaiah 44:5).

MISCELLANEOUS PAPERS.

Like the verse on page 141, this was found in her Manuscript Book N° VIII, one of her "Verses on Texts." See pages 559–568 of Volume I of the Havergal edition.

SICKNESS FROM GOD'S HAND.

(Written after reading a contrary statement.)

I. Direct Testimony from Scripture.

Leviticus 26:16: In threatening consumption and the burning ague, God says, "I also will do this unto you."

Deuteronomy 7:15: "*The Lord* ... will put none of the evil diseases of Egypt ... upon thee; but will lay them upon all them that hate thee."

Deuteronomy 28:27: "*The Lord* will smite thee with the botch of Egypt," etc. Ver. 35: "*The Lord* shall smite thee in the legs and in the knees," etc. Ver. 59–61: "Then *the Lord* will make thy plagues wonderful, ... sore sicknesses, and of long continuance, moreover *He* will bring upon thee all the diseases of Egypt, ... also every sickness and every plague ... them will *the Lord* bring upon thee."

2 Samuel 12:15: "*The Lord* struck the child, and it was very sick."

2 Chronicles 21:18: "*The Lord* smote him in his bowels with an incurable disease."

"And the *Lord* smote the king, so that he was a leper unto the day of his death" (2 Kings 15:5).

Psalm 32:4: "For day and night *Thy* hand was heavy upon me." It is an evident description of fever.

Psalm 38:2: "*Thine* arrows stick fast in me, *Thy* hand presseth me sore." The context again shows this to have been severe sickness.

Psalm 39:10: "Remove *Thy* stroke away from me; I am consumed by the blow of *Thine hand*." The consuming in this and next verse again describes the normal effect of sickness.

Isaiah 38:15: "Himself *hath done it*." This needs no comment, enough if it stood alone in the Bible!

Micah 6:13: "Therefore also will *I* make thee sick in smiting thee."

Acts 12:23: "The angel of *the Lord* smote him." (Herod.)

II. Indirect Testimony.

Psalm 41:3: "*Thou* wilt make all his bed in his sickness." Does not this tender, sympathetic, and continuous care in sickness militate against the idea that sickness is from Satan, and therefore "not to be remained under!"

Psalm 121:7: "*The Lord* shall preserve thee from *all evil*."

I will put the argument from this into two syllogisms.

(1) What is of Satan must be evil. God's people are preserved from *all evil*. *Therefore*, God's people are preserved from whatever is of Satan.

(2) God's people are preserved from whatever is of Satan. They are not preserved from sickness. *Therefore*, sickness is not of Satan.

2 Samuel 24:14, 15. David expressly says that in accepting the pestilence he is falling into the hand of *the Lord*. "And *the Lord* sent a pestilence upon Israel," etc.

Psalm 88:3, 4, 6. Ver. 3, 4, apparently imply sickness: "nigh unto the grave," "no strength"; but David follows it with "*Thou* hast laid me in the lowest pit, in darkness, in the deeps."

I suppose we all agree, and often tell others, that "*all* things," in Romans 8:28, really means "ALL things," sickness included; if we do, must we not equally say that in 2 Corinthians 5:18 "*all* things" really means ALL things, sickness included!

"Chastening," so far as I can recollect, is always spoken of as the act of God. But in Job 33:19 sickness is distinctly spoken of and stated to be chastening, *ergo,* from God. Also equally distinctly in Psalm 118:18, from God.

(In passing, what a wonderful parallel that passage, Job 33:19–28, has with James 5:14–16.)

Luke 9:1 : *Christ* gave them power and authority over all devils, *and* to cure diseases, *i.e. two separate* things.

There are several similar passages. The way in which sickness is mentioned four times in Matthew 25 does not seem to harmonise with the Satanic theory, though I cannot formulate it.

Similarly the mention in John 11:4.—Leprosy is the typical sickness, and the one of all others which one would *expect* to be referred to Satan, and the one over which Christ especially displayed His power; but so far as I recollect, it is never once spoken of in connection with the devil, but always inferentially as from *God Himself,* this being expressly stated in 2 Kings 15:5, already quoted. St. Paul would hardly have left Trophimus at Miletum sick, and spoken so very calmly of the fact, if he had believed *that* sickness to be from Satan, and "not to be remained under."

That Satan may be permitted in special cases to be the direct instrument of sickness, (*e.g.* Job, also the woman referred to in Luke 13:11), is a *very* different thing, and seems as clear as that he is not the usual and normal instrument. The *mass* of instances on the other side, and the plainest Bible statements, surely preclude this.

June 2, 1878.   F. R. H.

ARE *ALL* THE CHILDREN OF GOD?[1]

No text shows the affirmative. On the other hand:

I. It is distinctly stated that some are *not* the children of God. "They which are the children of the flesh, these are not the children of God" (Romans 9:8). "In this the children of God are manifest, and the children of the devil; whosoever doeth not righteousness is not of God, neither he that loveth not his brother" (1 John 3:10; John 8:41, 42, 44).

II. Distinct conditions are annexed to being or becoming, the children of God, which are manifestly not fulfilled by all.

First condition. *Believing* on the name of Christ and receiving Him. "But as many as received Him, to them gave He power to become the sons of God, even to them that believe on His name" (John 1:12). Also Galatians 3:26.

Second condition: *Love* to the Lord Jesus Christ. "Jesus said unto them, If God were your Father ye would love Me" (John 8:42).

Third condition. *Being led* by the Spirit. "For as many as are led by the Spirit of God, they are the sons of God" (Romans 8:14).

III. The children of God are constantly mentioned in contradistinction to others who are described as the children of a different father or power. See Romans 9:8; 1 John 3:10; Matthew 13:38; Ephesians 2:2, 3, 5, 6; Luke 16:8; and many other passages. Observe that when St. Paul called Elymas "child of the devil" (Acts 13:10), it is expressly said in ver. 9 that Paul was "filled with the Holy Ghost." I have looked out (with concordance) every place where "children" or "sons of God" occurs, and am struck with two facts.

1. That, even when not expressly stated to apply only to some and not to all, the same is *implied* in every case; *e.g.* Matthew 5:44, 45, "Love your enemies, bless them that curse you, do good to them that hate you, and pray for them which despitefully use you and persecute you; *That ye may* be the children of your Father which is in heaven," *not* "because" ye *are!*

2. That baptism is never once said to be the means of adoption, or of being or becoming, the children of God.

[1] Written after F. R. H.'s return from church, where *all* the congregation were addressed as being the children of God.

SIX ILLUSTRATIONS OF THE UNITY IN DIVERSITY OF THE HOLY SCRIPTURES.

(1) The system of typical persons, places, things, and events, all converging in the Person and offices of Christ.

(2) The steadily increasing light of prophecy, from the Seed (Genesis 3:15) to the Sun (Malachi 4:2).

(3) The gradual revelation of God Himself throughout the whole Old Testament, till Christ came, "God manifest in the flesh," and then the unfolding of that revelation throughout the New.

(4) The striking unity of conception in the allusions to creation in Job, Psalms, Proverbs, Ecclesiastes, and the prophets.

(5) The startling *contrasts* between Ecclesiastes and the Song of Solomon, suggesting evident design in their inspiration and juxtaposition.

(6) The connection of the Book of Proverbs with the *history* of the Old Testament and the *morality* of the New.

All of these (and many others) would be interesting to work out thoroughly. I take one only as a specimen—the last named.

I. The Book of Proverbs seems to be an epitome of the lessons to be learnt from the whole of Scripture history; or the history as a volume of illustrations of the Proverbs. Taking a single book (chosen haphazard), the Second of Chronicles, we find the following parallels. (This list is by no means exhaustive.)

2 CHRONICLES.	PROVERBS.		2 CHRONICLES.	PROVERBS.	
1:10	compare	4:5–7	10:6–13	compare	29:9
1:12	"	3:16	11:1–4	"	21:30
2:3	"	27:10	14:11	"	18:10
6:30	"	15:11	16:7–8	"	29:25
9:2	"	20:5	18:7	"	29:10
10:6	"	27:10	20:35	"	22:24, 25
10:7	"	15:1	20:37	"	13:20
23:13	"	11:10	29:36	"	16:1
24:17, 18	"	29:12	30:9–11	"	28:13
24:22	"	17:13	30:26	"	29:2
25:9	"	10:22	32:8	"	12:25
26:16	"	29:23	32:31	"	17:3
26:16	"	16:18	34:3	"	8:17
28:15	"	25:21	36:5, 9, 11	"	28:2

II. The morality of the Proverbs is identical with that of the New Testament. The precepts of the former *generally* occur as statements in the latter, and *vice versa*; *e.g.*:

Proverbs 3:9	compare	1 Corinthians 16:2
3:28	"	Matthew 5:42
8:13	"	Romans 12:9
10:12	"	1 Peter 4:8
11:12	"	Romans 12:16
12:20	"	Matthew 5:9
14:17, 29	"	James 1:19
18:12	"	James 4:10
19:11	"	Matthew 18:22
20:21	"	1 Timothy 6:9–11
21:4	"	Romans 14:23
24:29	"	1 Peter 3:9
28:21	"	James 2:1 (& *e.g.* Jude 16)

III. *Every* book in the New Testament has some parallel in Proverbs, some chapters (*e.g.* Romans 12, James 4) having parallels with nearly every verse.

Matthew 5:8	compare	Proverbs 22:11
Mark 12:33	"	21:3
Luke 12:24, 27	"	6:6
John 12:26	"	27:18
Acts 5:1–8	"	19:5, 9
Romans 12:16	"	3:7
1 Cor. 15:33	"	22:24, 25
2 Cor. 9:6	"	11:24, 25
Galatians 6:7–9	"	11:18, 22:8
Ephesians 4:31	"	4:24
Phil. 3:13, 14	"	4:25
Colossians 1:9, 11	"	24:5
1 Thess. 5:15	"	20:22
2 Thess. 3:11, 12	"	14:23
1 Timothy 6:17	"	11:28
2 Timothy 3:15	"	22:6

Titus 1:13	compare	Proverbs 15:32
Philemon 20	"	12:20
Hebrews 4:13	"	15:11
James 1:5	"	4:7
1 Peter 3:15	"	22:21
2 Peter 3:15	"	28:23
Galatians 2:11	"	28:23
1 John 3:22	"	15:29
2 John 11	"	17:15
3 John 10	"	10:8, 10
Jude 10	"	4:19
Revelation 3:19	"	3:11,12

INTERNAL EVIDENCE OF THE PROBABILITY THAT ST. PAUL WROTE THE EPISTLE TO THE HEBREWS.

I. Similarity of *style* with his other epistles.

1. The order of: first doctrine (chap. 1 to 11), then practice (chaps. 12, 13).

2. His continuous argument, yet parenthetical idiosyncrasy; *e.g.,* chap. 3:7–11, 4:7–10.

3. His manner of Old Testament quotations, resembling especially in this the Epistle to the Romans.

4. His way of drawing inferences from single words (as in Galatians 3:16); *e.g.,* "under" (Hebrews 2:8), "new" (8:13), "yet once more" (12:27).

5. His use of a postscript. Adaptation to those to whom he wrote. We could have been sure this epistle was *meant* for the Hebrews, just as we see the adaptation of the Romans.

II. Similarity as to favourite *words*; *e.g.* (1) "therefore" and "wherefore," his constant link between doctrine and practice. (2) His courteous "I beseech." (3) Christ as the "Son." (4) "Remember." (5) "Promise," etc., etc.

III. Similarity ("in diversity") of *topic*: (1) Faith; (2) Submission to authority, doing good to others, and other practical points.

IV. Miscellaneous evidence.

1. Negative.

(*a*) It was *not* by one of the twelve, and probably not by one who had personally "heard Him" while on earth. See Hebrews 2:3.

(*b*) It was apparently not by one who himself held definite rule or office in any church (chap. 13:7, 17).

(*c*) It was not by an obscure individual who required introduction, or apology, or credentials.

2. Positive.

(*a*) It was written by one who had been in bonds (Hebrews 10:34); (*b*) and who had been helped by those to whom he wrote (Philippians 4:14); (*c*) who had apparently had experience of reproach (chap. 13:13), and of "wanderings" (chap. 13:14); (*d*) who was intimately acquainted with Jewish laws and customs; (*e*) who had written longer epistles than this (chap. 13:22); (*f*) who was *in* Italy but only as sojourner (chap. 13:19, "restored to you"); (*g*) who was intimate with Timothy, using the term "brother," St. Paul's usual epithet in speaking *of* him (N.B. he speaks *to* him as "son"); (*h*) who rejoiced to acknowledge good in others (chap. 6:9), yet was faithful in reproof (chap. 5:12); (*i*) who seemed to feel and bear "the care of all the churches" (2 Corinthians 11:28); (*j*) who acknowledges God's grace in himself (Acts 23:1, and Hebrews 13:18).

V. Coincidences between the 13th chapter and the other Pauline epistles (not already mentioned).

Hebrews 13:1	.	.	.	.	.	1 Thessalonians 4:9
2	.	.	.	.	.	Romans 12:13
3	.	.	.	.	.	Philemon 1; Eph. 3:1; Col. 4:18
4	.	.	.	.	.	Ephesians 5:23–32
5	.	.	.	.	.	1 Timothy 6:9–11
– 2nd clause	.	.	.		.	1 Timothy 6:6–8; Philippians 4:11
– 3rd clause	.	.		.	.	Romans 8:35, 38, 39
6	.	.	.	.	.	2 Timothy 4:17, 18
7	.	.	.	.	.	1 Thessalonians 5:12
– 2nd clause	.	.		.	.	1 Corinthians 11:1
8	.	.	.	.	.	1 Corinthians 2:2
9	.	.	.	.	.	2 Timothy 4:3; 1 Timothy 4:16
– 2nd clause	.	.		.	.	2 Thessalonians 2:17

– 3rd clause	.	.	Romans 14
Hebrews 13:12 .	.	.	.	1 Corinthians 1:30
13 .	.	.	.	2 Corinthians 6:17
14 .	.	.	.	2 Corinthians 5:1; Philippians 3:20
15 .	.	.	.	Ephesians 5:20
– 2nd clause marg.	.	Romans 10:9, 10
16 .	.	.	.	Romans 12:13; Galatians 6:10
– 2nd clause	.	.	Philippians 4:18
17 .	.	.	.	1 Thessalonians 5:12
– 2nd clause	.	.	1 Corinthians 16:16
– last clause	.	.	1 Thessalonians 2:19, 20
18 .	.	.	.	2 Corinthians 1:11
– 2nd clause	.	.	2 Corinthians 1:12; 2 Timothy 1:3
– 3rd clause	.	.	2 Thessalonians 3:8, 9; Romans 12:17
19 .	.	.	.	Romans 1:10; 15:30–32; Philemon 22
20, 21	.	.	.	1 Thess. 5:23; 2 Thess. 2:16
20, 1st clause	.	.	Romans 15:33, 16:20; Philipianns 4:9
– 2nd clause	.	.	Romans 8:11; 1 Corinthians 6:14
21 .	.	.	.	Col. 1:10; Php. 2:13; Eph. 2:10, 1:19, 3:13
22 .	.	.	.	Philemon 9
– 2nd clause	.	.	Galatians 6:11
23 .	.	.	.	2 Timothy 4:21

VI. Coincidences between this Epistle and St. Paul's speeches in Acts. It seems remarkable that these occur most in the *later* speeches, those which are nearest to the date of the Epistle.

P.S.—I have only glanced at the "Acts" coincidences, and have not yet worked them out.

———————————

[Note: This was the end of *Starlight Through the Shadows*.]

The Voice from the Mercy Seat.

Num. 7. 89.

What to do with us? Everything — for Heb. 1. 2.

I. The Ark. II. The Mercy Seat. III. The Voice from it

I. The Ark. See Ex. 25. 10-16. "When we find it in the law, that law becomes gospel":

1. Shittim wood & gold — human & divine

2. "Overlaid — not 2 parts, separable, but all the wood overlaid with gold "perfect God & perfect man":

3. Crown round about. royalty; "throne of grace":

4. Rings & staves. 5. In Holy of holies, dark, no created light needed

II. 1. What for? To contain tables of law. Refer to last lesson. Ex. 40. 8.

2. Described & ordered & provided before law written Ex. 31. 18, & 32. 15, 16. So it foretold & provided before, Never a moment when it was not. (2) before law broken — God foresaw, so bef. He gave law it. He knew wd. be broken, Mediator & Substitute provided to keep it perfectly.

3. To contain second set of tables — first broken, never pieced together again Ex. 32. 19 — renewed set, Ex. 34. 1, 4; 28. Adam broke divine law, therefore 1st covenant ats an end. So have we, so no covenant of works avails. If one party breaks conditions, contract null. Therefore God renewed & placed in better hands — put into an Ark it. held it safe till all its required fully accomplished.

II. The Mercy Seat.

1. Gold only. Mercy God's prerogative, Mark 2:7.

2. Exact size — v. 17. as wide as It's whole nature — no wider, no mercy outs of It — see Heb. 10. 28, 29. II Cor. 5. 19.

3. Kept in place by crown. Sovereignty & kingly righteousness. "A God all mercy were a God unjust"

4. Covered tables of law. God shut up its curses"

This was the first page of F.R.H.'s handwritten manuscript, "The Voice from the Mercy Seat." See pages 148–151. Her sister Maria prepared this and many other manuscripts for publication after her death, invaluably preserving and disseminating Frances' works.

ADDENDA: 2 BIBLE STUDIES PUBLISHED IN *LETTERS*

These two lessons were published in the volume of *Letters by the Late Frances Ridley Havergal* edited by her sister, Maria V. G. Havergal (London: James Nisbet & Co., 1886), original book pages 272–275, pages 223–224 of Volume IV of the Havergal edition. These are similar to items near the end of *Starlight Through the Shadows* (see pages 142–179 of this book).

Deuteronomy 28:12: "The Lord shall open unto thee His good treasure."

Lesson I.—*The Good Treasure—The Unsearchable Riches of Christ* (Ephesians 3:8).

I. The Treasure itself. His, not ours, we have nothing, we are "poor" (Revelation 3:17). Consider the Riches of—1. Goodness; 2. Forbearance; 3. Longsuffering (Revelation 2:3); 4. Wisdom; 5. Knowledge (Colossians 2:3); 6. Grace (Ephesians 2:7); 7. Glory (Philippians 4:19), corresponding to our— (1) Sinfulness; (2) Provocations; (3) Repeated waywardness; (4) Foolishness; (5) Ignorance; (6) Spiritual need and weakness; (7) Immortal spirit.

How this treasure is purchased? (2 Corinthians 8:9). For whom?—1. The needy and poor (Revelation 3:17); 2. See context of Deuteronomy 28:12; 3. Christ's (1 Corinthians 3:21–23).

If Christ's, then all are yours.

II. The Promise itself. 1. Our need of the promise "shall open"; we cannot open ourselves: it is the Holy Spirit's office (John 16:14, 15). Some of us can bear witness, "I was blind, now I see," but cannot say Song of Solomon 2:16. Some can say 1 Peter 2:7. Praise Him! 2. The certainty of the promise "*shall* open." Do not say, "I hope He will"; come boldly and claim. Do not say "perhaps" when He says "shall" (Numbers 23:19). Faith is the key to this treasure; God *gives* it, it fits the lock of any promise. The Lord always responds to the claim of faith. He meets you with Matthew 7:7. There is always a promise at the back of everything: Expect and watch for the opening of the lock. (1) If opened to you, it will never be shut again, "He openeth and no man shutteth" (Revelation 3:7); (2) If opened, you will never come to the bottom—the riches are "unsearchable," always "more and more," "incorruptible"; now and through eternity, they are "the fulness of the Godhead." 3. If opened, we shall not care for other things, *e.g.* as they were opened to St. Paul (Philippians 3:8). 4. If opened, draw from it, be spiritual millionaires, use it, trade with it, the responsibility is great (1 Peter 4:10). What will you do with these riches this week?

Dwell on each word "THE LORD"—no human promiser, but God that cannot lie; "*shall*," fling this in Satan's teeth when tempted to doubt or to be negligent in search; *"open,"* it is never shut up from you; *"unto thee,"* really, personally, not merely to somebody else, or folks in general; *"His,"* not yours, all His very own, you had no right or claim to it; *"good,"* recollect it is seven-fold, perfection; *"Treasure"* even Jesus Himself, the Treasure of treasures, in all His fulness as your own Saviour, Friend, and King.

Lesson II.—*The Good Treasure.*

I. His Word. *His;* the value of the gift is enhanced by the giver. It is Christ's gift (John 17:14), and the Father's gift to Him (verse 8). *Treasure;* the value is relative and actual. *Relative,* " MORE than gold " (Psalm 19:10; 119:72, 127). If we really find treasure, we are glad (Psalm 119:162; Jeremiah 15:16).

A *test* to apply to ourselves in Psalm 1:2, "delight," and in Jeremiah 6:10, no delight. If there is no rejoicing in it, the treasure is not yet opened to us; this is the work of the Holy Spirit (John 14:26). The answer to the prayer Psalm 119:18 is Jeremiah 33:3. See Christ's own double opening, Luke 24:32, 45.

II. *Actual.* The value of the treasure is proved by what it will do for us. " Do not My words *do good,*" etc. What good?
1. We are born again by it (1 Peter 1:23).
2. Growth thereby (Psalm 1:2, 3) in grace and in knowledge (1 Peter 2:2; 2 Peter 3:18).
3. It gives light (Psalm 119:105).
4. It gives understanding.
5. It gives quickening (Psalm 119:50, 93).
6. It gives patience (Romans 15:4).
7. It gives comfort.
8. It gives hope.
9. It keeps from sin (outward) (Psalm 119:11).
10. It sanctifies (inward) (John 17:17).
11. It is profitable for, etc. (2 Timothy 3:15, 16).
12. It is able to save your souls (James 1:21).
13. The climax—by these ye become "partakers of the divine nature" (2 Peter 1:4).

Faith is the key of this treasure (1 Thessalonians 2:13); "worketh" all this "effectually in you that believe" (compare Hebrews 4:2: "Not mixed with faith").

Isaiah 55:11: "My word . . . shall prosper . . . whereto I sent it"—all this!

III. Responsibility attached to the Treasure. The command is Colossians 3:16 (connect 2 Corinthians 4:7). See the promise (Proverbs 8:21), "I will fill their treasures." They *bring forth* out of this good treasure things new and old (Matthew 12:35; 13:52).

ADDENDA: 7 BIBLE STUDY CARDS,
AND BIBLE STUDY OR OUTLINE

This Bible study card for December 30, first Sunday after Christmas, was likely written for December 30, 1877, and was found among Havergal manuscripts and papers, written in her handwriting. After this one, there are six more that were typewritten by her.

Dec 30. 1st Sunday after Xmas [Christmas]. Isa 42
Selected Text. 4th verse. He shall not fail [oe ? illegible] Isa 9.7 & I Cor 15.20. Connect with verse 16 "not forsake" and both with Joshua 1–5. Comp[are] Zeph 3.5. (Present Tense) with Psa[lm] 89.33. & Lam 3.22. Comp[are] Psa 38.10 & Psa 70.1 Josh 23.14 & I Kings 18 [? not sure of writing here] 18.56. Why? Thou art the same & Thy years shall not fail. Heb 1.12. Look out New Test. Fulfillment of the prophecies in verses 1.7 of Xt [Christ]
Sev illust of the form [illegible] promises in v.16
[illegible] 1 . John 9.35–38. 2 . Hosea 2–6.14
3 . Mic 7–8 I Pet 2.9. 4 . Gen 42.36 – 48.11.

[Note: The Greek letter X (chi) is the first letter of the Greek name Χριστόσ, Christ. When F.R.H. (who was either fluent or at least very proficient in reading the Greek New Testament) wrote "Xmas," that was an obvious shorthand for Christmas, and similarly "Xt" meant Christ.]

These six typewritten cards with Bible studies (and also one handwritten card) were found among Havergal manuscripts and papers. Though we definitely do not know the time these were written, they likely were between December 31, 1877 and January 5, 1878, because the typewriter was used, and we have a typewritten manuscript of her poem "The Song of a Summer Stream" which was written February 18, 1879. There is also an extant letter from "The Typewriter Company" in London (dated October 24, 1878, addressed to "Miss Havergal [either Maria or Frances], the Mumbles, Swansea") concerning the typewriter sent to them to be repaired. We do not know the occasion for these six Bible studies, and these six were the only ones found. These cards were typed in all capital letters, and the words written in by hand very much look like F.R.H.'s handwriting. These were almost surely written and typed by Frances.

Dec. 31. Monday. Isaiah 43. Selected text, verses. "<u>When thou passest through the waters</u>, <u>I will be with thee</u>" Parallel promise, Psa. 91.15; connect Matt. 28.20. & v. 5. Literal fulfilments, Ex. 14.29,30. Isa. 63.13. Josh. 3.17. Psa. 107.23–30. Jonah 2.3–5. Matt. 14.27. Acts 27.23. Spiritual fulfilments, 2 Sam. 22.5,17. Psa. 32.6. Psa. 66.12. Compare Psa. 84.6. Psa. [No reference was typed here.] Zec. 13.9. Acts 14.22.   See Psa. 29.3. & Cant. 8.7.

Notice in this chapter [Isaiah 43] 10 things that God has done for us., & 10 promises of what He will do. Contrast all these with verses 23–24. Connect verses 3, 11, & 25.

Evening Reading, Revelation 22. 10–21.

January 1. Tuesday. Isaiah 44.

Selected text, v. 23. "Sing, O ye heavens; for the Lord hath done it." i.e., hath redeemed us. Thus we begin the new year with note of praise. Psa. 52.9. Connect John 19.30. "Finished", Deut. 32.4. "Perfect"; & Psa. 111.3. "Honourable & glorious." See Ecc. 3.14. Compare Psa. 22.30,31. with Isa. 44.3 & 17, "seed" & "done."   "<u>Jehovah</u> hath done it." See v.6; Psa. 34.32; Psa. 111.9; Isa. 47.4; 63.17. Christ fulfilled it; Eph. 1.7; Heb. 9.18; I [sic as found typed] Gen. 1.30; I Pet. 1.18,19.

Take the words "Yet <u>now near</u>" in v.1, as keynote of the chapter and let the heart-reply be Psa. 85.8.

Contrast "my" & "their own" in verses 8,9.

Observe in this & the following chapters how often God declares that there is "none beside Him," "none else;" & notice the context in each case.

Evening Reading, Matthew 1.

Jan. 2. Wednesday morning. Isaiah 45.

Selected text, v.24. "Even to him shall men come." Literal fulfilment. John 3.26. Ten instances in 8th & 9th chapters of St. Matt.

Present Fulfilment. ["Present Fulfilment" was written in by hand, in F.R.H.'s handwriting.]

Those whom the Father gives, John 6.37. The Son draws, John 12.32. Results of coming; 1. acceptance, John 6.37. 2. rest, Matt. 11.28,29. 3. building up, I Pet. 2.3,4. 4. satisfaction, John 6.35. Let us reply with Jer. 3.22. Future fulfillment. Gen. 49.10. John 10.16. John 11.52. Isa. 60.6–8. Compare John 6.37,44,45, with John 7.37. & Rev. 22.17.

See in this chapter how many things are said about Jehovah, which are elsewhere said of Jesus Christ.

Evening Reading. Matt. 2. ["Evening Reading. Matt. 2." was written in hand by F.R.H.]

Jan. 3. Thursday morning. Isaiah 46.

Selected text, v.13. "I bring near my righteousness." Parallel, Isa. 51.5. Now [question mark typed and crossed out] 2 Cor. 5.21. "Near" to those that are "far", v.12. See Dan. 9.24, "bring in". Rom. 1.16,17. Contrast Isa. 64.6. Connect Isa. 45.24, "have I", with Isa. 61.10, "hath clothed", & Rom. 3.22. See Matt. 5.20, & Phil. 3.9. Connect Jer. 23.5 & I Cor. 1.30. Observe Rom. 10.3.

Contrast verses 4. & 7. Seal each prophecy with v.10, & each declaration & promise with last half of v.11.

Evening Reading, Matt. 3.

Jan. 4. Friday morning. Isaiah 47.

Selected text. "Thou that art given to pleasures, that dwellest carelessly." Compare 2 Tim. 3.4, "loving"; I Tim. 5.6, "living in"; Titus 3.3, "serving"; & Luke 8.14, "choked with". See I John 2.17. Contrast "thy pleasures", Psa. 36.8. Job 36.11. * Psa. 16.11. See Zeph. 2.15. Compare Ezek. 16.49. & Prov. 1.32, margin. See Isa. 32.9,10,11. Ezek. 39.6. Contrast "without carefulness", I Cor. 7.32. I Pet. 5.7.

Contrast the threats to Babylon with promises to Zion. E.G. v.1, with Isa. 52.2. v.5, "silent", with ch. 30.29; 35.10; &6. "Darkness", with ch. 60.19. "Shalt no more be called", with ch. 62.4. v.9, "loss of children" with ch. 54.1; 61.9. "widowhood" with ch. 64.4,5. And other contrasts.

Evening Reading, Matt. 4.

Jan. 5. Saturday morning. Isaiah 48.

Selected text, v.16. "Come ye near unto me." Contrast Exod. 10.12,21. Then see Heb. 12.18–24. "Ye are come," "to Jesus," See Num. 16.5; Jer. 30.21; & Psa. 65.4. Then compare Num. 16.5,7, & Lev. 10.3.; & see 2 Chron. 29.31.   Types.   Gen. 45.4,9,10,18,19.   Esther 5.2.   See Eph. 2.14; & Psa. 148.14. Therefore Heb. 10.22.

Notice God's reason for giving prophecies, vs. 3–7.

Contrast our character in v.8. with what He says He has done & will do through the rest of the chapter.

Observe the mention of the three persons of the holy trinity in one clause of v.16.

Evening Reading. Matt. 5.1–16.

These are comments on the two pages of notes written in F.R.H.'s handwriting, shown on pages 187 and 196 of this book. Frances wrote this in a letter dated October 23, 1878: "Just finishing reading Exodus—so strange and tantalizing that I never get the spiritual enjoyment out of that set of types that I really do out of the historical ones, though I know all the typical points. But Joseph! I am so sorry I touched that type in one or two chapters of *Royal Invitations,* for when reading Genesis four or five weeks back, I thought I should so like to do a little book like *My King or Our Brother,* and work that aspect of Christ with Joseph rather prominent, as David in *My King.*" (in *Letters by the Late Frances Ridley Havergal,* original book page 399, page 259 of Volume IV of the Havergal edition) After her death, a list was found in her desk, entitled "Work for 1879 'If the Lord will.' " (a facsimile copy of the list given on pages 208–209 of Volume III of the Havergal edition), and on the second page of that list she wrote "Our Brother; or Daily Thoughts for those who love Him." Apparently (we do not know with certainty) she was thinking of a 31-day book like the five Royal Books, and apparently (again, we do not know with certainty), these two pages written in Frances' handwriting may have been notes written in preparation for *Our Brother.* Faintly showing from the other side of the paper are typewritten words, so that apparently she wrote these notes on a used or scrap piece of paper. The first page of these notes is on page 187, and the second one is on page 196.

Gen. 27. 29. be lord over thy br.
Gen. 49. 8. Thou art he whom thy br. shall praise
Deu. 17. 15. King from among br.
Deu. 18. 15 Prophets from among br
I Sam 17. 17, 18. look how thy brethren fare
                    Joseph.
Gen. 37. 13. I will send thee unto them c. 45 & 5.
— 16. I seek my brethren
— 23 when J. was come unto his b. they stripped J.
4 2. 7 & 23 Jan. — knew his br. they knew not him
— — they knew not him.
— 21 verily guilt concerning our brother
— 24 - wept & returned & communed
— 25 - thus did he unto them
43. 16 these men shall dine with me
— 30 J. made haste &
44. 1. as much as they can carry.
45. 1 there stood no man with him while &c
— 3, 5 I am Joseph.
— 7. to save yr. lives by a gt. deliverance
— 15 after that his br. talked with him
— 16 fame thereof was heard
— 24 see that ye fall not out
— 26 Jo. is yet alive & is governor
46. 31. I will go up & shew P.
47. 2. presented them unto P.
47. 11 placed his father & br. in the best of the land
— 12. nourished his br
50. 15 - they said, J. will peradventure hate us.
— 21 comforted them & spoke kindly

Please read the paragraph at the bottom of page 186 for an explanation of this page
of notes in F.R.H.'s handwriting.

REVELATION 1:7 BEHOLD, HE COMETH.

This manuscript, written in F.R.H.'s handwriting, was found among other Bible studies or outlines, a number of them given at the end of *Starlight Through the Shadows*. Almost certainly this one has never been published until now.

Though she never wanted nor approached any position as "clergy," she prepared studies both for herself and for others to learn and grow. I think that few have had her knowledge of Scripture (others have, but few), and not a head knowledge with pride but from the Lord a heart knowledge with love. Her notes that Maria included at the end of *Starlight Through the Shadows*, especially her notes on the author of Hebrews and on the unity in diversity of Scriptures (pages 175–179 of this book), are examples, not wholly but partly showing what I mean. Far beyond her memorization (all the New Testament except the Book of Acts, all the Minor Prophets, Isaiah, all the Psalms, and also many other individual chapters, including chapters memorized in Hebrew), I think that she was intimately familiar with every page of Scripture and had a deep, vast knowledge—full of love.

This is an example of what she meant when she wrote of "searching" (searching the Scriptures)—which she so loved to do, and encouraged others to do. Scores of big baskets full can be gathered from examining her personal Bagster study Bible. This Bible has been photographed with a very high quality of resolution, and if the Lord wills, this should be published in its entirety as a facsimile Addendum to the Havergal edition.

F.R.H. loved the Author, and the Scriptures, His own and very words to us. After and from Him, she loved others and wanted them to know Him and to study, search, know His Word.

David Chalkley

Re. 1. 7. Behold, __He__ cometh . (Zc. 14. 20.)

I. __Who__ is coming ? Acts 1. 11. John 14. 3 - 7.
            Isa. 52. 6. Job 19. 27.

    Who shall see Him ?
   Rev 1. 7   }   Isa. 35. 5. }   I Cor . 13. 12. }
   Zech 12. 10 }   —   33. 17. }   Isa. 52. 8. }

II. __How__ is He coming ?

1 (With clouds . Rev. 1. 7.
2 {   —   shout - voice of arch. 1 Th. 4. 16
3 {   —   angels . Mat. 25. 31. "all" Dan 7. 10.
4 (—   them that sleep. I Thess. 4. 14.

1 (In His glory . Ps. 102. 16. Mat 25. 31. Rev. 1.
2 {   —   beauty. Is. 33. 17. II Thess 1. 10.
    beaut. v gt. Is. 4. 2.

III. __Why__ is He coming ?

1 (For judgment Ps. 98. 9. II Tim 4. 1. II Th. 1. 7. 8.
2 { — Salvation Heb. 9. 28. I Pet 1. 7-9.
3 (To receive His people I Jo. 14. 3.
4 { — reward them Rev 22. 13 crowns. II Tim 4. 8,
      Rev. 2. 10. I Pet 5. 3.

IV. __When__ is He coming ?

    Mark 13. 32, 36. I Th. 5. 2. John 16. 16.

Therefore . II Pet. 3. 11. Lu. 12. 36, 37. I Jo. 2. 28.
  [1] Watching   [2] Looking   [3] Waiting   [4] Loving
  Mark 13. 35 .   Tit. 2. 13. }   I Co. 1. 7. }   II Tim. 4. 8.
           Ph. 3. 20. }   II Th. 3. 5 }

No difference to us whether Col. 3. 4. or I Th. 4. 17.

__Then__, [1] Joy   [2] Reunion   [3] Likeness
    Jo. 16. 22   I Th. 4. 17   I Jo. 3. 2.
    Is. 66. 5.   II Th. 2. 1.   II Th. 1. 10 "in" m. w.
Rev 22. 20. Even so, come, Lord Jesus !

F.R.H.'s manuscript of this Bible study or outline.

Revelation 1:7 Behold, He cometh. (Exodus 14:20)

I. *Who* is coming? Acts 1:11 John 14:3 Isaiah 52:6 Job 19:27

    Who shall see Him?
Revelation 1:7   Isaiah 35:5   1 Corinthians 13:12
Zechariah 12:10   Isaiah 33:17   Isaiah 52:8

II. *How* is He coming?

    1. With clouds Revelation 1:7
    2. With shout, voice of archangel 1 Thessalonians 4:16
    3. With angels Matthew 25:31 "all" Daniel 7:10
    4. With them that sleep 1 Thessalonians 4:14

    1. In His glory Psalm 102:16 Matthew 25:31 Revelation 1: [Here Frances
       did not write the verse. (Possibly verses 6 and 7.)]
    2. In His beauty Isaiah 33:17 2 Thessalonians 1:10
       beauty & glory Isaiah 4:2

III. *Why* is He coming?

    1. For judgement Psalm 98:9 2 Timothy 4:1 2 Thessalonians 1:7, 8
    2. For salvation Hebrews 9:28 1 Peter 1:7–9
    3. To receive His people John 14:3
    4. To reward them Revelation 22:12 — 3 crowns 2 Timothy 4:8
        Revelation 2:10 1 Peter 5:3 [She meant 5:4.]

IV. *When* is He coming?

Mark 13:32, 36 1 Thessalonians 5:2 John 16:16

Therefore. 2 Peter 3:11 Luke 12:36, 37 1 John 2:28

1 Watching	2 Looking	3 Waiting	4 Loving
Mark 13:35	Titus 2:13	1 Cor. 1:7	2 Timothy 4:8
	Philippians 3:20	2 Thess. 3:5	

No difference to us whether Colossians 3:4 or 1 Thessalonians 4:17.

Then.   Joy   Reunion   Likeness
          John 16:22   1 Thessalonians 4:17   1 John 3:2
          Isaiah 66:5   2 Thessalonians 2:1   2 Thessalonians 1:10 " in "
                                                   [illegible?
                                                   "Greek word"?]

Revelation 22:20. Even so, come, Lord Jesus!

On the following pages is the identically same outline or study with the Scriptures quoted after the references.

F.R.H.'s manuscript of this next poem is found on pages 123–124.

What Thou Wilt.

Do what Thou wilt! Yes, only do
  What seemeth good to Thee:
Thou art so loving, wise, and true,
  It must be best for me.

Send what Thou wilt; or beating shower,
  Soft dew, or brilliant sun;
Alike in still or stormy hour,
  My Lord, Thy will be done.

Teach what Thou wilt; and make me learn
  Each lesson full and sweet,
And deeper things of God discern
  While sitting at Thy feet.

Say what Thou wilt; and let each word
  My quick obedience win; Let loyalty
and love be stirred
  To deeper glow within.

Give what Thou wilt; for then I know
  I shall be rich indeed;
My king rejoices to bestow
  Supply for every need.

Take what Thou wilt, belovèd Lord,
  For I have all in Thee!
My own exceeding great reward,
  Thou, Thou Thyself shalt be!

Frances Ridley Havergal

The Lord's Prayer.[1]
"Our Father."

"Our Father" – the Beautiful Gate of this temple. Only if we can say "Our Father," that the rest will be <u>prayer</u>. In one sense God is Father of all –Creation – Preservation. In another <u>not</u> – John 8:42. The former not enough for life or death. Heart craves personal caring, loving: Father. If <u>not</u> – we have made ourselves orphans – sinned – wandered – Luke 15.

<u>The Return</u> – <u>God</u> begins it – sovereignty of call to return. Ephesians 1:4

<u>How</u>? John 1:12. Jeremiah 3:19.

<u>Christ</u> has taken away all obstacles to adoption. Galatians 4:4–7. "that we might receive the adoption."

<u>Holy Spirit</u> seals the adoption. Galatians 4:6. Romans 8:15,17.

The <u>Tokens</u> of Adoption. Galatians 4:6. Hebrews 12:6,7.

<u>Privileges</u> of Adoption. Ephesians 2:18 Romans 8:17. Isaiah 63:16. John 20:17. I John 3:1,2. I Peter 5:7.

<u>Duties</u> of Adoption. I Peter 1:13. &ᶜ [etc.] obedience, love, submission.

<u>Conditions</u> of Adoption. II Corinthians 6:17.

<u>Promise</u> of Adoption. II Corinthians 6:18. Revelation 21:7.

---

[1] This is a transcription of an important manuscript—in F.R.H.'s handwriting—of her study or lesson on the Lord's teaching on prayer, "Our Father, Who art in heaven," found among her papers. Like all of the Havergal edition, diligent effort has been made here to be precisely faithful to the manuscript, but as this study was written with abbreviations, and apparently as notes primarily or only for Frances herself to use, not prepared for publication, minor changes have been added (such as abbreviated words spelled out fully, and missing periods added for uniformity among the outline points, the niceties that she clearly would have wanted in a published copy); withal, the handwritten text is copied very precisely here.

After years of wanting to include this manuscript study in the edition, but being unable understand the illegible parts of the manuscript (enough illegible to render the text inadequate or inappropriate to publish, though truly valuable to publish), and very near the end of the completion of the edition, Mrs. Trudy Kinloch looked at a copy of the manuscript and was able to understand what was previously indecipherable, graciously and quickly providing the missing parts. Sincere thanks are expressed to her, and also to a colleague who referred me to her, Dr. Digby L. James, whose decades-long research and preparation of *The Complete Works of George Whitefield* is so very valuable, and who has been genuinely kind and helpful to me in the Havergal work since we first met in 2002.

"Which art in heaven." Isaiah 57:15.

"Hallowed be Thy name." illustrate. <u>Follows</u> naturally from <u>Our</u> F. Test of love – gladness at "speaks good of name", pain at contrary. Promise – Malachi 1:11. in full

"Thy Kingdom come"

Three "kingdoms" referred to in various places – avoid confusion –

1. Inward – Luke 17:20,21..
2. Millennial – Jeremiah 23:5, 6.
3. Heavenly – II Timothy 4:18.

I. Inward. <u>What</u> is it? Romans 14:17.
This cannot be without a <u>King</u> – Jesus. Is He <u>our</u> King? Contrast Luke 19:14 with David, Psalm 84.3 "<u>my</u> King".
If King – obedience & subjection. John 14:15 & John 2:6. [F.R.H. likely meant John 2:5 here.] but then I John 5.3.   II Corinthians 10:5.
If King – power &ᶜ all on our side. illus. Abyssinian War. [In 1868, a huge force was sent to rescue a captured missionary, etc.]
Seek – Matthew 6:33.
<u>Are</u> we in? make sure – if not, in kingdom of Satan.

II. Millennial. Psalm 72.4. Revelation 20:6
"Jesus shall reign" &ᶜ [F.R.H. is likely referring to Isaac Watts' hymn "Jesus shall reign where 'man' er the sun doth his successive journeys run."]
Behold thy King cometh. [Zechariah 9:9; Matthew 21:5; John 12:15]
His people share it. Daniel 7:27. II Timothy 2:12.
If He reigns in us now, we reign with Him then.

III. Heavenly. Revelation 11:15. Isaiah 33:17. I Corinthians 15:25,28.

"Thy Will be done".

Generally only thought of in connection with suffering, e.g. I Peter 4:19.
Christ's example. Matthew 26:42.
But Ephesians 5:17. "understanding <u>what</u>".

I. God's will <u>for</u> us. His will as His nature – <u>love</u>. Ephesians 1:5, 6, 11, 12. John 6:39,40. John 17:23,24. Luke 12:32.

II. His will <u>in</u> us. I Thessalonians 4:3. & 5:18.
Sovereignty Daniel 4:35 – cf. [compare] I John 5:14.
Promises – John 17:17. Matthew 7:21.
What makes a † [symbol of cross, possibly or likely shorthand for Christian]
What is His <u>will</u> that we shd [should] <u>do</u>? Ephesians 6:6. I Peter 2:15
Example of doing [His] will. John 4:34. Hebrews 10:7
Hebrews 10:36.   Psalm 103:20-21.
Psalm 143:10.
Hebrews 13:20. [F.R.H. likely also meant Hebrews 13:21.]

"Give us this day"

I. Literal bread. At the Fall curse linked with bread Genesis 3:19 Xt [Christ (from Greek Χριστόσ)] "turned it into blessing". He gave prayer & promises abt [about] it.
<u>Has</u> fulfilled it. Psalm 37.25.
He never taught prayer for riches, bec. [because] not true happiness — Xt's [Christ's] teaching always for our happ. [happiness]. I Timothy 6:9–10. Proverbs 30:8. I Timothy 6:8.
Promises Isaiah 33:16. I Peter 5:7. Matthew 6:25-34. Philippians 4:19.
Crowns all with Exodus 23:25.
Jesus <u>hungered</u>. [Matthew 4:2]

II. Spiritual bread. 1. The Word. Deuteronomy 8:3. Matthew 4:4. Jeremiah 15:16.
    2. Christ. John 6.33-35.
Bread – sustains life – gives strength.
Whatever can be done without, bread can't [bread can't be done without].
Must be <u>eaten</u> & become part of ourselves. Canticles [Song of Solomon] 5:1.
Hunger. Luke 15:17. Matthew 5:6.
Promises Joel 2:26. Isaiah 65:13. Luke 2:53. [This was a mistake, and F.R.H. almost certainly meant Luke 1:53.] Revelation 7:16,17.

"Forgive us" &^c

Exodus 34:6–7. Psalm 130:4.
Psalm 32:1.

Psalm 103:3,12. Micah 7:18–19.
Isaiah 1:18. & 44:22. & 55:7.
Jerermiah 31:34 & Hebrews 8:12.   Daniel 9:9.
Acts 5:31. 10:43. 13:38.   Colossians 1:14.
Mark 2:5. I John 2:12.
     Proverbs 28:13. Mark 1:4.
          Hosea 14:1–4.

Proverbs 19:16. Matthew 18:21–35. Mark 11:25.
Luke 6:37. & 17:4.   Ephesians 4:32.
Colossians 3:13.

"Lead us not" &^c

Temptation – 1. Different for each.
     2. Repeated (Hebrews 12:1) or Varied.
     3. Open or Subtle.

I. From Satan for ill. James 1:13. I Chronicles 1:21. [This looks like Chr.,
especially when compared with reference to Chr on the next manuscript page,
but contextually I Chronicles 1:21 does not mention temptation; neither does
I Corinthians 1:21. This was likely a slip of the pen. F.R.H. may possibly or
likely have meant II Chronicles 21:1.] Matthew 26:41. I Corinthians 10:13.
James 4:7. I Peter 5:8. Ephesians 6:11–15.

II. From God for good (trial.) II Chronicles 32:33. [This is another human
mistake in F.R.H.'s notes. The Scripture that she was thinking of has not yet
been found.] Genesis.22:1. [surely referring to all of Genesis 22:1–19] & Hebrews 11:17. Deuteronomy 8:2. Job 23:10. Zechariah 9:13. I Peter 1:6,7. I
Peter 4:12.
Christ tempted – 1. – By Satan Matthew 4 & Luke 4.   2.– By wicked men.
Matthew 16:1 & 22:35 &^c &^c.   Manifold – Luke 22:28. Hebrews 2:18. &
4:15.
Promise James 1:12. Rom. 8:35–37.

[The manuscript was left incomplete, ending with Romans 8:35–37. This is an
example—a glimpse—of F.R.H.'s "searching the Scriptures."]

Prov. 17. 17. a brother is born for adversity

Pr. 18. 24. friend thats sticketh closer

Cant. 8. 1. O thats Thou wert as my brother

Math. 12. 50. the same is my br. & sister

Gen. 4. 10. The voice of thy brother's blood

Ex. 28. 1. Aaron thy brother (priesthood)   Lev. 21. 10.

Lev. 25. 35. 37. duties to a brother fulfilled

Deut. 15. 11. ditto   by Xt.

Lev. 25. 25. redeem thats wh. thy. b. sold.

Lev. 25. 47. – if he – – sell himself

Ex. 2. 11. Moses … looked on their burdens

De. 33. 24. acceptable to his brethren

Jud. 11. 3. fled from his brethren

I. Sam 16. 13. anointed him in the midst of br.

I Sam. 22. 1. br. went. to him at Adullam

II I Ch. 5. 22 br. came to comfort him

Mi. 5. 3. remnant of his br. shall return

Heb. 2. 17 – made like his br.

Ex. 4. 18. let me go & return to my br.

I Sam 30. 23. Ye shall not do so, my br.

II Sam 19. 12 Ye are my br

Ps. 22. 22 & Heb. 2. 12 I will declare … unto my br.

Ps. 69. 8 I am become a stranger to my br.

Matt. 25. 40 done it unto least of these my br

Matt. 28. 10 & John 20. 17 – go tell my br.

Please read the paragraph at the bottom of page 186 for an explanation of this page of notes in F.R.H.'s handwriting.